Field Guides to Finding a New Career

Science

The Field Guides to Finding a New Career series

Accounting, Business, and Finance

Advertising, Sales, and Marketing

Arts and Entertainment

Education

Engineering, Mechanics, and Architecture

Film and Television

Food and Culinary Arts

Health Care

Hospitality and Personal Care

Human Services

Information Technology

Internet and Media

Law and Justice

Nonprofits and Government

Outdoor Careers

Public Safety and Law Enforcement

Real Estate

Science

Sports Industry

Travel and Transportation

Science

By Angela Libal

Ferguson Publishing
An imprint of Infobase Publishing

Field Guides to Finding a New Career: Science

Ferguson
An imprint of Infobase Publishing
132 West 31st Street
New York, NY 10001

Library of Congress Cataloging-in-Publication Data

Libal, Angela.
    Science / by Angela Libal. — 1st ed.
        p. cm. — (Field guides to finding a new career)
    Includes bibliographical references and index.
    ISBN-13: 978-0-8160-7999-5 (hardcover : alk. paper)
    ISBN-10: 0-8160-7999-4 (hardcover : alk. paper)
    1. Science—Vocational guidance—Juvenile literature. I. Title. II. Series.
    Q147.L53 2010
    500—dc22

                                                    2009051359

Ferguson books are available at special discounts when purchased in bulk quantities for businesses, associations, institutions, or sales promotions. Please call our Special Sales Department in New York at (212) 967-8800 or (800) 322-8755.

You can find Ferguson on the World Wide Web at http://www.fergpubco.com

Produced by Print Matters, Inc.
Text design by A Good Thing, Inc.
Illustrations by Molly Crabapple
Cover design by Takeshi Takahashi
Cover printed by Bang Printing, Brainerd, MN
Book printed and bound by Bang Printing, Brainerd, MN
Date printed: March 2010

Printed in the United States of America

10 9 8 7 6 5 4 3 2 1

This book is printed on acid-free paper.

Contents

Introduction: Finding a New Career vii

How to Use This Book ix

Make the Most of Your Journey xi

Self-Assessment Quiz xv

Chapter 1   **Laboratory Technician** **1**

Chapter 2   **Atmospheric Scientist** **13**

Chapter 3   **Geoscientist** **24**

Chapter 4   **Grant Writer** **36**

Chapter 5   **Health and Safety Technician** **47**

Chapter 6   **Chemist and Materials Scientist** **57**

Chapter 7   **Science Teacher** **67**

Chapter 8   **Environmental Scientist** **78**

Chapter 9   **Technical Writer** **90**

Chapter 10   **Food Technologist** **101**

Appendix A   Going Solo: Starting Your Own Business 111

Appendix B   Outfitting Yourself for Career Success 125

Index 137

Introduction: Finding a New Career

Today, changing jobs is an accepted and normal part of life. In fact, according to the Bureau of Labor Statistics, Americans born between 1957 and 1964 held an average of 9.6 jobs from the ages of 18 to 36. The reasons for this are varied: To begin with, people live longer and healthier lives than they did in the past and accordingly have more years of active work life. However, the economy of the twenty-first century is in a state of constant and rapid change, and the workforce of the past does not always meet the needs of the future. Furthermore, fewer and fewer industries provide bonuses such as pensions and retirement health plans, which provide an incentive for staying with the same firm. Other workers experience epiphanies, spiritual growth, or various sorts of personal challenges that lead them to question the paths they have chosen.

Job instability is another prominent factor in the modern workplace. In the last five years, the United States has lost 2.6 *million jobs*; in 2005 alone, 370,000 workers were affected by mass layoffs. Moreover, because of new technology, changing labor markets, ageism, and a host of other factors, many educated, experienced professionals and skilled blue-collar workers have difficulty finding jobs in their former career tracks. Finally—and not just for women—the realities of juggling work and family life, coupled with economic necessity, often force radical revisions of career plans.

No matter how normal or accepted changing careers might be, however, the time of transition can also be a time of anxiety. Faced with the necessity of changing direction in the middle of their journey through life, many find themselves lost. Many career-changers find themselves asking questions such as: Where do I want to go from here? How do I get there? How do I prepare myself for the journey? Thankfully, the Field Guides to Finding a New Career are here to show the way. Using the language and visual style of a travel guide, we show you that reorienting yourself and reapplying your skills and knowledge to a new career is not an uphill slog, but an exciting journey of exploration. No matter whether you are in your twenties or close to retirement age, you can bravely set out to explore new paths and discover new vistas.

Though this series forms an organic whole, each volume is also designed to be a comprehensive, stand-alone, all-in-one guide to getting motivated, getting back on your feet, and getting back to work. We thoroughly discuss common issues such as going back to school, managing your household finances, putting your old skills to work in new situations, and selling yourself to potential employers. Each volume focuses on a broad career field, roughly grouped by Bureau of Labor Statistics' career clusters. Each chapter will focus on a particular career, suggesting new career paths suitable for an individual with that experience and training as well as practical issues involved in seeking and applying for a position.

Many times, the first question career-changers ask is, "Is this new path right for me?" Our self-assessment quiz, coupled with the career compasses at the beginning of each chapter, will help you to match your personal attributes to set you on the right track. Do you possess a storehouse of skilled knowledge? Are you the sort of person who puts others before yourself? Are you methodical and organized? Do you communicate effectively and clearly? Are you good at math? And how do you react to stress? All of these qualities contribute to career success—but they are not equally important in all jobs.

Many career-changers find working for themselves to be more hassle-free and rewarding than working for someone else. However, going at it alone, whether as a self-employed individual or a small-business owner, provides its own special set of challenges. Appendix A, "Going Solo: Starting Your Own Business," is designed to provide answers to many common questions and solutions to everyday problems, from income taxes to accounting to providing health insurance for yourself and your family.

For those who choose to work for someone else, how do you find a job, particularly when you have been out of the labor market for a while? Appendix B, "Outfitting Yourself for Career Success," is designed to answer these questions. It provides not only advice on résumé and self-presentation, but also the latest developments in looking for jobs, such as online resources, headhunters, and placement agencies. Additionally, it recommends how to explain an absence from the workforce to a potential employer.

Changing careers can be stressful, but it can also be a time of exciting personal growth and discovery. We hope that the Field Guides to Finding a New Career not only help you get your bearings in today's employment jungle, but set you on the path to personal fulfillment, happiness, and prosperity.

# How to Use This Book

Career Compasses

Each chapter begins with a series of "career compasses" to help you get your bearings and determine if this job is right for you, based on your answers to the self-assessment quiz at the beginning of the book. Does it require a mathematical mindset? Communication skills? Organizational skills? If you're not a "people person," a job requiring you to interact with the public might not be right for you. On the other hand, your organizational skills might be just what are needed in the back office.

Destination

A brief overview, giving you an introduction to the career, briefly explaining what it is, its advantages, why it is so satisfying, its growth potential, and its income potential.

You Are Here

A self-assessment asking you to locate yourself on your journey. Are you working in a related field? Are you working in a field where some skills will transfer? Or are you doing something completely different? In each case, we suggest ways to reapply your skills, gain new ones, and launch yourself on your new career path.

Navigating the Terrain

To help you on your way, we have provided a handy map showing the stages in your journey to a new career. "Navigating the Terrain" will show you the road you need to follow to get where you are going. Since the answers are not the same for everyone and every career, we are sure to show how there are multiple ways to get to the same destination.

Organizing Your Expedition

Fleshing out "Navigating the Terrain," we give explicit directions on how to enter this new career: Decide on a destination, scout the terrain, and decide on a path that is right for you. Of course, the answers are not the same for everyone.

Landmarks

People have different needs at different ages. "Landmarks" presents advice specific to the concerns of each age demographic: early career (twenties), mid-career (thirties to forties), senior employees (fifties) and second-career starters (sixties). We address not only issues such as overcoming age discrimination, but also possible concerns of spouses and families (for instance, paying college tuition with reduced income) and keeping up with new technologies.

Essential Gear

Indispensable tips for career-changers on things such as gearing your résumé to a job in a new field, finding contacts and networking, obtaining further education and training, and how to gain experience in the new field.

Notes from the Field

Sometimes it is useful to consult with those who have gone before for insights and advice. "Notes from the Field" presents interviews with career-changers, presenting motivations and methods that you can identify with.

Further Resources

Finally, we give a list of "expedition outfitters" to provide you with further resources and trade resources.

Make the Most of Your Journey

There is a special excitement that comes from working in the sciences. You have the unique opportunity to study and manipulate the fundamental materials and principles of our physical world; to apply the most exciting and groundbreaking knowledge and discoveries to your day-to-day work; and, in rare and fantastic moments, to add to these discoveries and enrich this body of knowledge.

Career choices in science are as diverse as the disciplines themselves. The skill sets these careers call for are similarly diverse, yet many overlap. For example, laboratory technicians, health and safety technicians, and food technologists all call upon knowledge of biology, chemistry, and mathematics. Many careers detailed in this book involve rugged, outdoor fieldwork, especially atmospheric scientist, geoscientist, and environmental scientist. These careers are very closely linked in their research and specific duties. Scientists specializing in any of them will frequently find themselves working in teams with the others. Jobs like grant writer and technical writer, on the other hand, involve a great deal of time researching in print rather than in a laboratory. Most work is conducted individually and in front of a computer. Communication skills are invaluable in both of these careers.

If you love science, you are virtually guaranteed to find a career that will suit your interests within this cornucopia of applied techniques and training. If you are passionate about the outdoors, nature, and wildlife conservation, and would love to spend your working life on location in some of the most beautiful wilderness areas of the world, you may be a future environmental scientist. If you love working outdoors, and have a penchant for comparing and contrasting quantitative data, a career in geoscience could be beckoning you. Each career includes many possibilities, from camping deep in forests and scaling rock formations to traversing glaciers and diving to reefs. Both environmental science and geoscience require extensive, interdisciplinary training, but in each case your training will be rewarded by a career filled with breathtaking natural wonders. You will work directly with natural resources, where your passions can truly effect change for the better.

If your interests are focused on a smaller scale, and you are excited by the idea of studying and analyzing specimens in a laboratory all day, one of the many technician or technologist careers may be a fit for you. Perhaps you like to travel and sleuth for clues through all kinds of environments: combined with a passion for safeguarding human health, these interests could be melded into a career as a health and safety technician; or, combined with a passion for applied research, a career as a laboratory technician. Maybe you possess technical focus and are exhilarated by the thought of donning a white coat and goggles and spending hours over a microscope, but would also like to get down and dirty on the farm or in a test kitchen. If so, employment as a food technologist could be simmering in your future.

Some science careers embrace a broad spectrum of possibilities. Atmospheric scientists may work in areas as remote and rugged as those populated by geoscientists and environmental scientists. In this role you could spend your time stationed in a national forest or with a geologic survey out in the field, studying air and water conditions with the end goal of preserving natural habitats. A little closer to civilization, you could be employed managing plans for disaster preparedness or consulting on flood control to preserve human habitations and transportation infrastructure. Alternatively, your career voyage could deliver you to a research facility stationed on a boat in the open ocean, providing an early warning system for disastrous storms. Your weather station could also be a busy office located in a bustling urban airport, feeding weather forecasts to local news media.

If your passion is for teaching rather than research or an applied technical vocation, there are many different options to choose from. If you love children and are gifted with an ability to transform rote information into exciting, interactive adventures, teaching at the primary or secondary level may be your calling. Tutoring services may provide part time work with more academic freedom than a full time classroom. If your approach is more dynamic and interactive, and you are committed to restoring educational excellence in the sciences, public schools across the nation are facing a shortage of qualified science teachers. Perhaps you subscribe to a more specific philosophy of education and work best in small, intimate settings. Private schools, as well as publicly funded but privately operated charter or magnet schools, often have innovative openings for people with a science background. Teaching at the postsecondary level is another option, and possibilities lie in wait not only for those whose dream is to be a science teacher, but for those in any scientific discipline who have earned a master's degree or a doctorate.

Perhaps you have passion that is communicable, and are not averse to using it to gain funds for causes to which you and your employers are personally committed. Grant writing combines personal charisma with an intense belief in a cause, and transforms these through the discipline of professional writing into fund-raising for all types of scientific, educational, and philanthropic projects. As a grant writer, you must have excellent writing skills. Furthermore, you must be able to communicate a vision, to enflame the imaginations of those who work at funding agencies so they can see the benefits of your plan and help it blossom into reality by ample application of grant monies. A career in technical writing, by contrast, combines well-honed writing and teaching skills with the ability to conduct impeccable research in person, in print, and online. As a technical writer your primary job is to be a translator between the specialists who design products, such as engineers and developers, and the non-specialists who will be using them. In comparison to the other careers listed in this book, grant writing and technical writing do not require a scientific or technical background.

Requirements for entering careers in science exist on a continuum. Some require minimal training combined with experience earned on the job. Positions you can enter with an associate's degree include laboratory technician, where you will be working in a laboratory; and health and safety technician, where you will also be working in different occupational facilities inspecting a wide variety of conditions and hazards. Earning a higher degree in these fields can help further advancement to positions such as technologist or laboratory manager. Food technology is a related field with related degree requirements: one can enter at the technician level with an associate's degree, though advancement will require a bachelor's or even master's degree. If you have an extensive employment history in a similar occupation, you may be able to enter your newly chosen field by having a vocational certificate rather than a degree.

A bachelor's degree will outfit you for entry into the world of chemistry or materials science. Advancement from this point can be gained through on-the-job experience, as you prove your talent, knowledge, accuracy, and efficiency. A bachelor's degree is also the minimum requirement for most teaching positions at the primary and secondary level.

Still other positions—the fieldwork-intensive scientist positions, especially—require a master's degree. While a very few low-level positions may be available if you have a relevant bachelor's degree, the vast majority will require advanced degrees. These are fields that are currently undergoing change. They are becoming extremely competitive, and while expertise could formerly be proven by your performance on the job, the new trend is for you to prove yourself in advance with educational credentials. Geoscientist is such a position, as are atmospheric scientist and environmental scientist. Broad interdisciplinary training at both the undergraduate and graduate levels are what makes a prospective scientist employable in these competitive fields.

Whatever your career goals and educational aspirations, finding a new vocation in the scientific field involves packing the basic necessities: awareness, planning, and research. After this it takes the courage to set foot into the unknown. Outfit yourself with a basic understanding of the possible paths, traveler, and you will be on your way to your new adventure!

Self-Assessment Quiz

I: Relevant Knowledge

1. How many years of specialized training have you had?
   - (a) None, it is not required
   - (b) Several weeks to several months of training
   - (c) A year-long course or other preparation
   - (d) Years of preparation in graduate or professional school, or equivalent job experience

2. Would you consider training to obtain certification or other required credentials?
   - (a) No
   - (b) Yes, but only if it is legally mandated
   - (c) Yes, but only if it is the industry standard
   - (d) Yes, if it is helpful (even if not mandatory)

3. In terms of achieving success, how would you rate the following qualities in order from least to most important?
   - (a) ability, effort, preparation
   - (b) ability, preparation, effort
   - (c) preparation, ability, effort
   - (d) preparation, effort, ability

4. How would you feel about keeping track of current developments in your field?
   - (a) I prefer a field where very little changes
   - (b) If there were a trade publication, I would like to keep current with that
   - (c) I would be willing to regularly recertify my credentials or learn new systems
   - (d) I would be willing to aggressively keep myself up-to-date in a field that changes constantly

5. For whatever reason, you have to train a bright young successor to do your job. How quickly will he or she pick it up?
   (a) Very quickly
   (b) He or she can pick up the necessary skills on the job
   (c) With the necessary training he or she should succeed with hard work and concentration
   (d) There is going to be a long breaking-in period—there is no substitute for experience

II: Caring

1. How would you react to the following statement: "Other people are the most important thing in the world?"
   (a) No! Me first!
   (b) I do not really like other people, but I do make time for them
   (c) Yes, but you have to look out for yourself first
   (d) Yes, to such a degree that I often neglect my own well-being

2. Who of the following is the best role model?
   (a) Ayn Rand
   (b) Napoléon Bonaparte
   (c) Bill Gates
   (d) Florence Nightingale

3. How do you feel about pets?
   (a) I do not like animals at all
   (b) Dogs and cats and such are OK, but not for me
   (c) I have a pet, or I wish I did
   (d) I have several pets, and caring for them occupies significant amounts of my time

4. Which of the following sets of professions seems most appealing to you?
   (a) business leader, lawyer, entrepreneur
   (b) politician, police officer, athletic coach
   (c) teacher, religious leader, counselor
   (d) nurse, firefighter, paramedic

5. How well would you have to know someone to give them $100 in a harsh but not life-threatening circumstance? It would have to be...
    (a) ...a close family member or friend (brother or sister, best friend)
    (b) ...a more distant friend or relation (second cousin, coworkers)
    (c) ...an acquaintance (a coworker, someone from a community organization or church)
    (d) ...a complete stranger

III: Organizational Skills

1. Do you create sub-folders to further categorize the items in your "Pictures" and "Documents" folders on your computer?
    (a) No
    (b) Yes, but I do not use them consistently
    (c) Yes, and I use them consistently
    (d) Yes, and I also do so with my e-mail and music library

2. How do you keep track of your personal finances?
    (a) I do not, and I am never quite sure how much money is in my checking account
    (b) I do not really, but I always check my online banking to make sure I have money
    (c) I am generally very good about budgeting and keeping track of my expenses, but sometimes I make mistakes
    (d) I do things such as meticulously balance my checkbook, fill out Excel spreadsheets of my monthly expenses, and file my receipts

3. Do you systematically order commonly used items in your kitchen?
    (a) My kitchen is a mess
    (b) I can generally find things when I need them
    (c) A place for everything, and everything in its place
    (d) Yes, I rigorously order my kitchen and do things like alphabetize spices and herbal teas

4. How do you do your laundry?
    (a) I cram it in any old way
    (b) I separate whites and colors

(c) I separate whites and colors, plus whether it gets dried

(d) Not only do I separate whites and colors and drying or non-drying, I organize things by type of clothes or some other system

5. Can you work in clutter?

(a) Yes, in fact I feel energized by the mess

(b) A little clutter never hurt anyone

(c) No, it drives me insane

(d) Not only does my workspace need to be neat, so does that of everyone around me

IV: Communication Skills

1. Do people ask you to speak up, not mumble, or repeat yourself?

(a) All the time

(b) Often

(c) Sometimes

(d) Never

2. How do you feel about speaking in public?

(a) It terrifies me

(b) I can give a speech or presentation if I have to, but it is awkward

(c) No problem!

(d) I frequently give lectures and addresses, and I am very good at it

3. What's the difference between *their*, *they're*, and *there*?

(a) I do not know

(b) I know there is a difference, but I make mistakes in usage

(c) I know the difference, but I cannot articulate it

(d) *Their* is the third-person possessive, *they're* is a contraction for *they are*, and *there* is a deictic adverb meaning "in that place"

4. Do you avoid writing long letters or e-mails because you are ashamed of your spelling, punctuation, and grammatical mistakes?

(a) Yes

(b) Yes, but I am either trying to improve or just do not care what people think

   (c)   The few mistakes I make are easily overlooked
   (d)   Save for the occasional typo, I do not ever make mistakes in usage

5.   Which choice best characterizes the most challenging book you are
      willing to read in your spare time?
      (a)   I do not read
      (b)   Light fiction reading such as the Harry Potter series, *The Da Vinci
            Code*, or mass-market paperbacks
      (c)   Literary fiction or mass-market nonfiction such as history
            or biography
      (d)   Long treatises on technical, academic, or scientific subjects

V: Mathematical Skills

1.   Do spreadsheets make you nervous?
      (a)   Yes, and I do not use them at all
      (b)   I can perform some simple tasks, but I feel that I should leave them
            to people who are better-qualified than myself
      (c)   I feel that I am a better-than-average spreadsheet user
      (d)   My job requires that I be very proficient with them

2.   What is the highest level math class you have ever taken?
      (a)   I flunked high-school algebra
      (b)   Trigonometry or pre-calculus
      (c)   College calculus or statistics
      (d)   Advanced college mathematics

3.   Would you rather make a presentation in words or using numbers
      and figures?
      (a)   Definitely in words
      (b)   In words, but I could throw in some simple figures and
            statistics if I had to
      (c)   I could strike a balance between the two
      (d)   Using numbers as much as possible; they are much more precise

4.   Cover the answers below with a sheet of paper, and then solve the
      following word problem: Mary has been legally able to vote for exactly
      half her life. Her husband John is three years older than she. Next year,

their son Harvey will be exactly one-quarter of John's age. How old was Mary when Harvey was born?
(a) I couldn't work out the answer
(b) 25
(c) 26
(d) 27

5. Cover the answers below with a sheet of paper, and then solve the following word problem: There are seven children on a school bus. Each child has seven book bags. Each bag has seven big cats in it. Each cat has seven kittens. How many legs are there on the bus?
(a) I couldn't work out the answer
(b) 2,415
(c) 16,821
(d) 10,990

VI: Ability to Manage Stress

1. It is the end of the working day, you have 20 minutes to finish an hour-long job, and you are scheduled to pick up your children. Your supervisor asks you why you are not finished. You:
(a) Have a panic attack
(b) Frantically redouble your efforts
(c) Calmly tell her you need more time, make arrangements to have someone else pick up the kids, and work on the project past closing time
(d) Calmly tell her that you need more time to do it right and that you have to leave, or ask if you can release this flawed version tonight

2. When you are stressed, do you tend to:
(a) Feel helpless, develop tightness in your chest, break out in cold sweats, or have other extreme, debilitating physiological symptoms?
(b) Get irritable and develop a hair-trigger temper, drink too much, obsess over the problem, or exhibit other "normal" signs of stress?
(c) Try to relax, keep your cool, and act as if there is no problem
(d) Take deep, cleansing breaths and actively try to overcome the feelings of stress

3. The last time I was so angry or frazzled that I lost my composure was:
    (a) Last week or more recently
    (b) Last month
    (c) Over a year ago
    (d) So long ago I cannot remember

4. Which of the following describes you?
    (a) Stress is a major disruption in my life, people have spoken to me about my anger management issues, or I am on medication for my anxiety and stress
    (b) I get anxious and stressed out easily
    (c) Sometimes life can be a challenge, but you have to climb that mountain!
    (d) I am generally easygoing

5. What is your ideal vacation?
    (a) I do not take vacations; I feel my work life is too demanding
    (b) I would just like to be alone, with no one bothering me
    (c) I would like to do something not too demanding, like a cruise, with friends and family
    (d) I am an adventurer; I want to do exciting (or even dangerous) things and visit foreign lands

Scoring:

For each category...

For every answer of *a*, add zero points to your score.
For every answer of *b*, add ten points to your score.
For every answer of *c*, add fifteen points to your score.
For every answer of *d*, add twenty points to your score.

The result is your percentage in that category.

Laboratory Technician

Laboratory Technician

Career Compasses

Get your bearings on what it takes to be a successful laboratory technician.

Relevant Knowledge of laboratory procedures (40%)

Mathematical Skills to properly perform tests and correctly interpret results (30%)

Organizational Skills and careful attention to detail to avoid dangerous and costly mistakes (20%)

Ability to Manage Stress and successfully function in a job that has no safe margin of error (10%)

Destination: Laboratory Technician

If the hands-on science of working with samples in a laboratory appeals to you, you may be cut out to be a laboratory technician. To enter the field of laboratory technology you must have a good grasp of laboratory procedures, analytical skills, good judgment, and excellent attention to detail. The modern laboratory technician is called on to prepare samples, run biological assays, interpret test results, test medical equipment, and communicate results and findings clearly and accurately.

Mathematics and computers must not intimidate you. A background in mathematics up to and including statistics is essential. A basic ability to work with computers, including the ability and willingness to learn new programs and procedures, is a must as more laboratory procedures become automated.

Knowledge of proper laboratory safety procedures and protocol is essential. More than 50 percent of laboratory technicians are employed in hospitals, with the remaining portion employed by physicians' offices, medical and diagnostic laboratories, medical equipment manufacturers, and educational or government facilities. The vast majority of samples you will be working with are of a biological nature, such as blood and other bodily fluids, as well as microorganisms, and many of them are potentially infectious. You may also be working with hazardous chemicals. To work safely and ethically as a laboratory technician, you must not only be aware of safety precautions, but also be willing and able to put them into use each and every time you enter your workplace.

Most sampling and testing work has a physical element: you must be able to accurately measure and mix small amounts

Essential Gear

Brush up on your math skills. If you have not taken a math class in years, and your current employment does not involve doing a lot of math, some independent study or a math course at your local community college may help you. Most of the tests run by laboratory technicians in all fields involve math, and all sampling involves accurate measurement, usually in the metric system. If you are a little rusty, start with the level you currently feel comfortable at and work your way up. Even the most advanced levels of math build step-by-step on the simpler ones. Work through it carefully and you will find that math is easy!

of substances and to clearly read the results of tests. Steady hands are a must, and, since many biological assays show results as a change in sample color, so is clear and normal color vision. Squeamishness is a drawback in a laboratory environment. Biological samples include blood, urine, feces, tissue, and infectious agents, and laboratory technicians are often the ones who take the samples and always the ones who prepare them. There are a large number of specialties grouped under the title "laboratory technician." For example, a phlebotomist has a very different job from someone who tests insulin shunts for quality control, whose job is very different from the technician's who prepares slides of *E.*

coli cultures. Research the various possibilities and ask questions about the actual responsibilities of any job you are offered.

Working with medical samples and equipment involves a great deal of responsibility. Diagnosis and treatment of disease—in other words, the health and lives of patients—may depend on correct sampling, testing, and interpretation of results. If you work in research and development or quality control for medical equipment, the lives of consumers may depend on your accuracy and good judgment here as well. At the very least a technician's error can lead to costly retrials for a company, hospital, or research program. There is no room for mistakes, and you must have the ability to work quickly and accurately under this pressure at all times.

With the majority of laboratory technicians employed in health care, another consideration for this career is the hours. Work hours often resemble those of other health care personnel, with long day or night shifts, and may include regularly working weekends, evenings, and holidays. There is generally not a lot of down time in a laboratory, so you must be comfortable spending your time at work "on the go."

Essential Gear

Investigate licensing requirements. Different states have different requirements for technicians working in laboratories. Some require licensing through the state's Department of Health or Board of Occupational Licensing, some require accreditation through various recognized professional organizations, some require specific certification programs, and some may not have a licensing requirement at all. If you are interested in a specific field (phlebotomy, histotechnology, cytotechnology, medical research assistant), look into the requirements in your state. State requirements may determine the type of degree or certificates you need to acquire.

As with many highly specialized, technological fields, laboratory technician jobs typically offer a steady, reliable livelihood to those with the proper qualifications and abilities, but this is by no means a get-rich-quick field. The median annual income for entry-level laboratory technicians, as of 2006, is $32,000. Higher incomes come with higher positions that require a master's degree or higher. A technician job can be the first step on a higher-paying career path, but if advancing up that path is your ultimate goal, an advanced degree combined with extensive work experience is necessary.

Laboratory technology is a fast-growing field, and with rising world population and continual development of new tests, testing methods, and medical equipment, it is expected to remain so. The need for well-educated workers with a background in math and science means that, so far, the demand for laboratory technicians has consistently exceeded the supply. This is a field that offers many options for immediate employment to candidates with the proper skills, motivation, and education.

You Are Here

Set yourself on the path to becoming a laboratory technician.

Are you new to laboratory science? If you have no science experience, go back to school. An associate's degree with a major in medical technology, the biological sciences, or chemistry will speed you on your way. This degree plus any specific certification programs (for example, phlebotomist) will technically qualify you for most entry level positions, but unless you already have related work experience, preference may be given to candidates with a bachelor's degree in medical technology or the life sciences. This higher degree can put you on track for supervisory positions and positions with more complex analytical, research, and development roles. If you wish to eventually work creating or modifying procedures and techniques or developing research programs yourself, a bachelor's degree will give you an excellent start. If you hope to someday be in charge of an entire facility, you will need a master's degree or higher in medical technology, the biological sciences, chemistry, management, or education.

Do you work in a related field? If you already have experience working in the sciences, you are much more likely to be able to get on-the-job training. Many companies hire laboratory technicians on a temp-to-hire basis. If you have a science, medical, or education background, check out local temporary employment agencies and register with ones who handle companies and facilities seeking laboratory assistants. A simple entry-level or temporary job preparing samples could be your foot in the door to a more complex laboratory technician job. Meanwhile, look into current local and federal regulations. Laws such as the Clinical Laboratory Improvement

Act may require that anyone performing certain procedures have a certain level of formal education. If your degree is in another field, now is the time to look at associate's degree programs in the sciences. If you already have experience working in a hospital or other health care facility, there may be specialized accreditation and certification programs in place to ease your way. If you have served in the Armed Forces working with health care or data analysis, you may also already qualify for some certification.

Do you have a degree in the sciences? If you have a science background, you may already be prepared to begin your job search. Investigate the requirements for specific openings and obtain any necessary additional certification. Consider your desired career path. If you hope to advance in the field to laboratory technologist (with more complex duties than a technician), supervisor, or director, go back to school. If you currently have an associate's degree, consider applying your credits to a bachelor's degree. If you already have a bachelor's degree in the sciences, consider returning for a master's or doctorate in medical technology, biology, physiology, chemistry, management, or education.

Navigating the Terrain

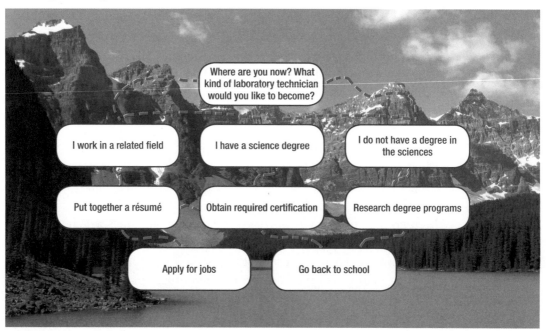

Organizing Your Expedition

Before you set out, know where you are going.

Decide on a destination. Most laboratory technicians are employed by hospitals where they process samples for the diagnosis of disease, but this is not the only employment option. Laboratory technicians also assist in research. If this idea interests you, institutions from pharmaceutical companies to agricultural service organizations to universities may hold possibilities for your future. Perhaps interacting directly with patients—taking blood or other samples—appeals to you, or you are interested in the development of new medical devices, procedures, or treatments. Running tests and analyzing data may be your strong suit. On the other hand, you may find that the processing of slides and samples suits you well. Consider whether your ultimate goal is to be a laboratory technician, or if you see this as a stepping-stone down a more complicated science career path. If it is the latter, finding the appropriate academic programs and working on an advanced degree will be just as important at this point as landing that first laboratory technician job.

Scout the terrain. Consider the options in your area. What facilities are hiring laboratory technicians? If you live in an urban area, you may have a wide variety of corporations, health care organizations, government agencies, and universities to choose from. If you live in a rural area your options may be more limited. If the options in your area do not suit your career goals, consider whether you are willing to adjust your goals or move for the right job.

Find the path that's right for you. Consider your interests and strengths, as well as your boundaries and limitations. If you cannot stand the thought of animal experimentation, for example, a pharmaceutical research laboratory is probably not for you. If you are passionate about public health, you may be happy processing swabs all day at your local clinic. Be realistic about your desires and abilities, strengthen your educational background where necessary, and seek out employment options that lead to your ultimate career goals where you feel your talents can shine.

Notes from the Field

Jennifer Moraca
Laboratory technician, quality control
Cypress, California

What were you doing before you decided to become a laboratory technician?

I was teaching. I taught seventh and eighth grade science (and also high school summer school science). I was working on an intern credential while getting my master's in education, through the Teach for America Program.

Why did you change your career?

Honestly, I found that teaching was not for me. I was teaching under very stressful conditions at an underperforming school, with very little training, and I did not like the amount of work. I taught six classes a day, had over 200 students, and then would have to go home and plan lessons, correct papers, and write tests. I really wanted a job that I did not have to take home as much (although I have never been really good about leaving work at work).

How did you make the transition?

I finished the semester then left my job and graduate school. I applied through various temporary agencies until I got a job working as a lab tech in a very large and well-known lab company. It only took a few weeks, but at the time I was not being very choosy. I would recommend being more selective—choose a field that interests you, and ask a lot of questions about the work you will be doing. My first tech job was little more than sample prep work and involved no real thought or analysis. I eventually left that job for one where I do a lot more thinking and analyzing data and trending data. It is much more challenging and offers much more room for growth.

My first tech job was a temp-to-hire job, which is how many labs hire technicians. It is an okay situation for the most part, but I prefer to be directly hired through a company, not through an agency. Many lab companies post jobs online, and not just through the big job search engines. Check the individual Web sites (which is how I found my current job, which I enjoy much more).

What are the keys to success in your new career?

Seek out work. In my experience, it is easy for lab techs to let themselves just perform their day-to-day duties, but that leads to stagnation and a lack of growth. Seek out ways to improve your process or ways to be involved with larger processes outside of your department. Ask for more responsibility, because it is easy for people to see you as "just a tech" who is only there to do your day-to-day work.

Think like a scientist. I currently work as Quality Control Technician at a medical device manufacturing facility. I run assays on our products to assess that they work correctly. Thinking scientifically about how the assays work helps immensely with troubleshooting and new product development. Be familiar with GLP, GDP, GMP (Good Lab Practice, Good Documentation Practice, Good Manufacturing Practices). Most labs that are in any way government regulated (which is most labs in general, but particularly medical, clinical, food manufacturing, etc) will follow these practices because it is mandated by the International Organization for Standardization and the Food and Drug Administration and you will have to be able to follow them.

If the only lab experience you have is from school, [it] pretty much does not count. In the corporate lab world, corporate experience is all that counts. This can be very frustrating, but it is a fact. Just be as confident in your lab technique as possible.

One of the biggest challenges I have faced is that people often assume lab techs do not really know what they are doing. There is an assumption that we do our work (running assays, etc) without really understanding it. But I have found that definitely not to be true. Both tech positions I have held required at the minimum a bachelor's in some science field, and everyone has completely understood their work. Often suggestions I have made or potential problems I have pointed out have been initially ignored (even though they were later found to be right) because I was "just a tech." This is something I still struggle with, because I often feel like I have more potential than given credit for. Seeking out work is a big remedy to this—the more you do and do competently, the more opportunities will open to you.

Another frustrating aspect, at least in the corporate side of things (I do not work in academia and never have, so I cannot speak for that

(continued on page 10)

Notes from the Field

(continued from page 9)
side) is the constant conflict between business and science. Many times, upper managers are not scientists, and want things that cannot be done. This is a really frustrating conflict, because it leads to competing goals, in the sense that they want to meet financial goals and marketing deadlines, but science does not always follow their schedule. It is important to be able to stand by your data and be confident in your technique. (This is from a QC stand point—as a I am QC lab tech. I sometimes get results that lead to thousands of dollars of products being scrapped because they are faulty. Consistent lab technique that I am confident in is key here. I have to be able to produce similar results on a retest, so that we can confirm that the product is indeed bad, and it is not a technician error)

Go back to school. Consider the level of schooling you will need. If you are already involved in science, health care, or education but need additional certification, research certificate programs at local community colleges, medical vocational schools, or trade and technical schools. If you are already a health care worker or a veteran, look for expedited and continuing education programs geared to people transferring to your new career from your current field. If you have a bachelor's degree or higher in an unrelated field, look into associate's degree programs in medical technology or the sciences at your local community colleges. Investigate available laboratory technician job openings, and see if your chosen educational program will allow you to continue working at your current job or to begin seeking entry-level laboratory positions while you are in school. If you have decided to pursue a bachelor's degree or higher, check out laboratory and research assistant work-study opportunities at your college or university. You may be able to begin your work experience as part of your course of study.

Landmarks

If you are in your twenties . . . If you have decided that you want to become a laboratory technician, seek a degree in the sciences and consider specialty certification. If you are an undergraduate, determine your options at your current school. Does it offer majors in medical technology, life sciences, chemistry, or specialized laboratory technician programs? If not, seek out an institution that will offer you the appropriate degree(s). If you wish to eventually advance to a higher position, consider a master's degree program in one of the life sciences or chemistry, medical technology, education, or management.

If you are in your thirties or forties . . . You may need to begin your career change by seeking a second degree or additional certification. Investigate educational options as well as the requirements of available job openings. Seek out temporary employment agencies that handle jobs in your chosen field and enroll in appropriate programs of study. Build a schedule that accommodates your work hours, career, and educational goals.

If you are in your fifties . . . If you are planning a career as a laboratory technician, you should already be working in a related field (science, health care, data analysis, education) or willing and able to return to school to acquire at least an associate's degree in the sciences. If you are working in a related field, find out if there are specialized certification or supplemental education programs that will take your current work experience into consideration.

If you are over sixty . . . Any applicable work experience will help you. Consider the advice for other age groups, and keep in mind that the more related experience you have on your résumé, the better. Math, science, and computer skills will go a long way to ease your transition. You will be competing with fresh college graduates who have the most up-to-date technological training, so if there is any question about your math, science, or computer competency, seek out applicable continuing education courses or an appropriate degree program.

Further Resources

The **National Accrediting Agency for Clinical Laboratory Sciences** provides a list of accredited and approved educational programs in the clinical laboratory sciences within the United States. The Web site has a feature that will search for programs by state or by educational institution, and covers a wide variety of clinical laboratory specialties. http://www.naacls.org

The **National Credentialing Agency for Laboratory Personnel** offers exams for certification in various laboratory fields. It also provides lists of necessary qualifications for different specialties, as well as a career networking database. http://www.ncaworks.nca-info.org

The **Clinical Laboratory Management Association** is an international professional association for laboratory workers that provides career information regarding various aspects of the laboratory sciences field from continuing education programs to legislative action updates to career networking. http://www.clma.org

The **Accrediting Bureau of Health Education Schools** accredits programs at institutions of higher education in the allied health care fields. The Web site also provides a directory of accredited programs and institutions, and updates on current industry and employment trends. http://www.abhes.org

Atmospheric Scientist

Atmospheric Scientist

Career Compasses

Get your bearings on what it takes to be a successful atmospheric scientist.

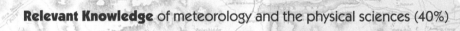

Relevant Knowledge of meteorology and the physical sciences (40%)

Communication Skills to share findings with colleagues, employers, or the public (20%)

Ability to Manage Stress in a fast-paced environment with long hours (20%)

Mathematical Skills to analyze and interpret data and track and predict weather patterns (20%)

Destination: Atmospheric Scientist

Weather affects human activities in a vast number of ways. Some of these impacts are the result of specific, extreme events, such as drought on agriculture, floods on buildings and transportation, or hurricanes on shipping. Others are subtle and constant, such as rainfall patterns on crops or grazing land; seasonal temperature on building standards; wind patterns on fire safety measures; and atmospheric conditions on radio, cellular, or landline communications. If you are fascinated by the Earth's atmosphere, climate, weather patterns, ocean, and geography, your forecast may hold a career in atmospheric science. Atmospheric scientists study past and present weather patterns in order to assess their impacts on human beings and our environment, and to predict future weather patterns and prepare for future impacts.

Atmospheric scientists must have an excellent understanding of the physical sciences. A good working grasp of basic physics is essential, including thermodynamics, electricity and magnetism, and the study of light, optics, and radiation. In addition to this, any background knowledge of physical sciences is helpful. Disciplines included in this category are oceanography, limnology and hydrology, geography and environmental science, astronomy, and climatology. Chemistry is also an important subject for atmospheric scientists, and excellent math and computer skills are critical.

Essential Gear

Get media-friendly. If you intend to pursue a career as a broadcast meteorologist, make sure you are media-savvy and camera-ready with excellent communication skills. Courses in broadcast journalism and speech will help you become competitive for career placement in this narrow and highly selective market.

Though all atmospheric scientists are considered "meteorologists," only a tiny minority fill the most visible role of television weather forecaster. Most atmospheric scientists work in industries where weather strongly affects human activities, such as agriculture, fishing, aerospace, transportation, communications, and shipping; and for gas, water, and power companies. In the United States, many atmospheric scientists are employed by the National Weather Service, or by government agencies such as the Forest Service, Bureau of Land Management, Defense Department, and other public and private organizations involved in forestry, defense, pollution control, and environmental research.

Under the umbrella term of "meteorologist" are several more specific job descriptions. Operational meteorologists study the physics of weather systems. These are the specialists who actually forecast the weather using mathematical processes and with the aid of satellites, weather balloons, Doppler radar, and computers. Physical meteorologists study the physical characteristics of the atmosphere itself and the formation of weather systems. Synoptic meteorologists work in research and development for new and improved ways of forecasting the weather.

Climatologists study the weather patterns of the distant past as well as the present in order to predict long-term variation in weather. Climatology studies are applied within the agriculture and construction industries, and findings may affect land use, infrastructure such as dams and levees, and safety and climate control elements in building design. Environmental meteorologists study human impacts on weather systems, including urban microclimates, impacts of air and water pollution, and how human activities may affect climate trends.

Most meteorologists involved in weather forecasting and research work in weather stations. These are the facilities that collect data from tools such as weather balloons and broadcast this data to the employing agencies, research facilities, radio stations, or television studios. The type of agency determines whether a single meteorologist or a research team is employed, and whether the station is located in an urban, rural, or remote area. A meteorologist working in air transportation, for example, would likely be working in a group at an urban weather station located in or near an airport. One involved in tracking weather systems for a shipping company or agricultural service might work at a rural weather station, and one working for the Forestry Service or Bureau of Land Management might be stationed in a remote location within a national forest or on other public lands. A broadcast meteorologist might work at any type of weather station in association with an urban or rural television or radio studio.

Essential Gear

Get a head-start with a volunteer position or internship. If you hope to work for a government agency, one of the surest ways to get noticed is through volunteer work. A number of government agencies that employ meteorologists also have numerous volunteer positions available, including the Bureau of Land Management, National Park Service, Department of Agriculture, Forest Service, National Oceanic and Atmospheric Administration, and Department of Fish and Game. Volunteering for these departments is a great way to make contacts and to get to know their inner workings, as well as to contribute in a way that can give you a great deal of personal satisfaction.

While a master's degree or doctorate may be necessary for higher-level and research positions, a bachelor's degree will allow you to enter the field of atmospheric science. The major you should choose will depend on the options available at colleges or universities in your area.

Very few schools offer a degree specifically in meteorology or atmospheric science, but a larger number offer courses in these fields within their science departments. If a degree in meteorology is unavailable, academic entry into the atmospheric sciences can be gained through a degree in physics, mathematics, engineering, oceanography, earth or environmental science, geography, or agricultural science plus appropriate meteorology and hydrology-related coursework.

Career openings in atmospheric science are limited but can be quite lucrative. The available number of government positions for meteorologists is currently predicted to decline due to a halt in the construction of new weather stations and the typically long tenure of persons employed in these positions. Some faculty positions teaching meteorology-related courses are open at colleges and universities for those with advanced degrees and teaching credentials. Very few positions as broadcast meteorologists (television and radio weather forecasters) are expected to become available. By far the fastest growing segment of the atmospheric science business is within private industry forecasting weather, conducting research to improve weather forecasting accuracy, studying pollution impacts, and monitoring emissions for compliance with federal regulations. This segment of the industry is expected to continue growing with excellent employment prospects for qualified individuals. As of May 2006, the median annual income for atmospheric scientists was approximately $77,000, with a typical starting salary ranging from $35,000 to $36,000. Those employed by the U.S. government were in a slightly higher income bracket, earning on average $84,882.

You Are Here

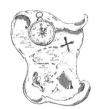

You can begin your journey to becoming an atmospheric scientist from several different locales.

Are you new to the sciences? If you are new to the sciences, and do not have a degree in mathematics or engineering, you will need to return to school to earn a bachelor's degree in meteorology or in a related field with a meteorology concentration. Consider the area of atmospheric science you would like to specialize in, as well as the type of job you wish to have once you have earned your degree. Would you rather work in a remote location monitoring weather conditions for environmental concerns? Perhaps you should consider coursework in agriculture or forestry. Would you prefer to work in a fast-paced, urban office setting? You may wish to consider additional coursework in broadcast journalism or look toward a career monitoring the weather for airlines, utility companies, or shipping. If research strongly appeals to you, it may do you well to consider an advanced degree and to look into openings within government departments, research universities, and other scientifically oriented enterprises.

Do you have a related degree? If you already work in the sciences, now is the time to add relevant coursework to your résumé. If you have an associate's degree in any of the physical sciences or mathematics, apply those credits to a bachelor's degree in meteorology, hydrology, engineering, mathematics, physics, or any of the physical sciences. Be sure to include relevant coursework in atmospheric science, and in broadcast journalism if you hope to become a media weather forecaster. If you already have a bachelor's degree in the sciences, mathematics, physics, or engineering, enroll in a program that will give you the necessary meteorology and hydrology coursework and consider returning to school for a master's degree or doctorate. If you already have an advanced degree in a related field, investigate job openings to determine what additional academic work or experience you will need to become competitive in this field. In rare cases relevant experience may substitute for a degree. If you have already worked in a related field for a number of years and have experience analyzing weather systems (for example, in engineering, forestry, agriculture, or infrastructure work such as levee design and repair), but do not have a related degree, investigate the actual requirements for job openings and consult with the agencies and facilities doing the hiring to predict where you may need to shore up any employability weaknesses.

Do you work in broadcast journalism? If you have experience in broadcast journalism, a move to broadcast meteorology may already be visible on your horizon. Determine the types of academic training and experience you still need and return to school if necessary. Use the contacts you already have within the media industry to increase your chance of earning a broadcast meteorology position. If possible, learn all that you can about how to succeed from personal contacts currently working in

Navigating the Terrain

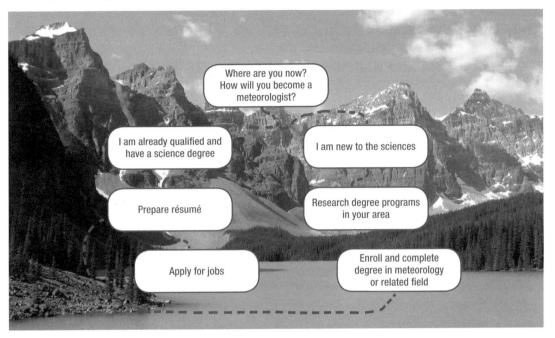

Where are you now?
How will you become a
meteorologist?

I am already qualified and
have a science degree

I am new to the sciences

Prepare résumé

Research degree programs
in your area

Apply for jobs

Enroll and complete
degree in meteorology
or related field

the field. If your intention is to move to an atmospheric science discipline unrelated to broadcasting, personal contacts in broadcast meteorology may still give you helpful advice about the types of academic programs and entry-level positions you should pursue to make your dreams a reality.

Organizing Your Expedition

Before you set out, know where you are going.

Decide on a destination. What type of atmospheric scientist would you like to become? Consider your strengths as well as your interests. Does your skill set pair atmospheric science with engineering and mathematical ability? Consulting on building construction and safety, transportation routes, or land use may be your strong suit. Are you deeply concerned about wildlife or the environment? You may wish to seek a job related to pollution control, emissions testing, forestry, wildlife

Notes from the Field
Eric Boldt
Warning coordination meteorologist
Oxnard, California

What were you doing before you decided to become an atmospheric scientist?

Attempting to become an electrical engineer. I changed majors midway through college.

Why did you change your career?

I was struggling with the math and physics needed for my engineering degree and was losing interest, so I switched to atmospheric science. Turns out the math and physics requirements were the same if not worse for a degree in meteorology.

How did you make the transition?

After my second year in college I transferred to a different university that had a B.S. degree in atmospheric science.

What are the keys to success in your new career?

Work experience, good communication skills, flexibility, and networking. The majority of atmospheric science careers involve a good deal of rotating shiftwork. Unless you are destined to become a manager one day, you will need to be prepared to work many nighttime hours and holidays, as well as overtime hours when significant weather impacts your area. Success will occur if you are proactive and energetic about new tasks and projects. It is also important to be flexible in moving to a different part of the country when a promotion becomes available.

management, or agriculture. Does the life of a television weather forecaster seem glamorous to you? You may be called to seek out one of the few and highly competitive jobs as a broadcast meteorologist. As you continue your adventure in meteorology, consider how the atmospheric sciences relate to various fields of human endeavor and the broad range of employment options. You may wish to investigate openings with the National Weather Service, but also with the Department of Parks and Recreation and the Forest Service; with broadcast media, but also with agricultural extension services, airlines, transportation and shipping companies, utilities, fishing industries—anywhere where the weather impacts human activity!

Scout the terrain. If you need to earn a bachelor's degree, fill in the meteorological gaps in your educational résumé, or return to school for an advanced degree, investigate which schools in your area offer relevant courses of study. If you are lucky enough to live near an institution that offers a degree in meteorology, hydrology, or the atmospheric sciences, look into enrollment requirements. If these majors are unavailable in your area, look for schools with science departments that offer related programs plus meteorology coursework. If no schools in your area offer relevant coursework, consider whether you are willing to move to pursue your education. Investigate the number of weather stations in your area and the possibilities for employment. What industries dominate locally? What is their need for weather forecasting and tracking? What types of positions are available, and how great is the demand? If there are few openings for someone with the education you are working to attain, consider whether moving to a different area where your skills will be in higher demand is the right choice for you.

Find the path that's right for you. If your current employment is unrelated to atmospheric science, consider how much time and effort you are willing and able to invest in switching careers. You will need to have at least a bachelor's degree in an appropriate field. If you do not yet have one, or yours is in an unrelated field, determine the extent of schooling you will need to commit in oder to fulfill employment requirements. If you already have a degree in the sciences, mathematics, physics, or engineering, or if you have a great deal of experience in a related field, you may be several steps ahead in the game, and a master's degree or doctorate could put you on the path to higher earning potential. Consider carefully whether you prefer solitude or teamwork, a fast-paced environment and hectic hours to a more typical workday, and work in a profit-motivated industry, government agency, environmental organization, or research facility. Your answers will help you to determine the types of jobs to seek out, and the locations in which to seek them.

Go back to school. Determine the type of programs and coursework that are necessary and available to achieve your goals. The American

Meteorological Society publishes a list of atmospheric science programs offered by colleges and universities in the United States at both the undergraduate and graduate levels. Decide which area you wish to specialize in and seek out programs that offer relevant education and training. The National Weather Service is the largest employer of meteorologists in the United States and publishes a list of courses required for employment.

Landmarks

If you are in your twenties . . . If you have decided you want to be a meteorologist, the first step is to gain an education in atmospheric science. If you are an undergraduate, determine whether you can take required courses at your current institution. If so, enroll in relevant classes. If not, transfer to a school that offers atmospheric science majors or related majors plus atmospheric science courses. If you have a specialty in mind, take additional courses in that area. If you are unable to transfer and your current institution does not have atmospheric science courses, major in oceanography, geography, environmental science, forestry, agricultural science, physics, engineering, or mathematics while looking into additional or advanced degree programs at other institutions. If you are not currently enrolled in school, apply for admittance to schools offering relevant programs.

If you are in your thirties or forties . . . You will need to set out on your career path by fulfilling any additional educational requirements. If you have a related degree, complete any necessary coursework in meteorology and your chosen specialty, or seek out an advanced degree program in the atmospheric sciences. If you do not have a related degree, go back to school to earn one. Decide whether you need to and are able to return to school part time or full time, whether you can continue working while attending classes, and whether you will have good job prospects in your current area or will need to relocate.

If you are in your fifties . . . If you intend to take on a new career in atmospheric science, you should already have experience in a related field, a related degree, and the ability to take any additional courses or enter graduate school, or the ability to return to school full time to earn an appropriate degree.

If you are over sixty . . . The advice to prospective meteorologists in their fifties also applies to you. Any work in related fields will put you at an advantage. If it has been a long time since you have used mathematics regularly, or if you have not yet mastered computer skills, you will need to put energy into these areas now.

Further Resources

The **American Meteorological Society** offers certification in consulting and broadcast meteorology to experienced, professional meteorologists. Qualification includes an exam, character references from within the atmospheric sciences field, and formal educational requirements. The society also publishes a list of accredited undergraduate and graduate atmospheric science programs available in the United States. http://www.ametsoc.org

The **National Oceanic and Atmospheric Administration** is the agency that employs U.S. government meteorologists through the National Weather Service. The administration's Web site provides information about career openings and educational requirements, as well as abundant reports on meteorological research. http://www.noaa.gov

The **U.S. Office of Personnel Management** is the official site for employment openings within the U.S. government. The Web site allows prospective employees to search for job openings in all departments by type of job and location. http://www.usajobs.opm.gov

Geoscientist

Geoscientist

Career Compasses

Get your bearings on what it takes to be a successful geoscientist.

Relevant Knowledge of the geological sciences (40%)

Organizational Skills to collect, collate, and interpret large amounts of data (25%)

Ability to Manage Stress while working at remote locations in extreme environments under difficult conditions and with limited facilities (25%)

Mathematical Skills to take measurements and collect, analyze, and interpret data (10%)

Destination: Geoscientist

Does your love for rocks set you apart from the crowd? You may have already laid the foundation for a career in geoscience. Geoscientists work in a variety of disciplines whose common focus is the physical characteristics of the Earth's land and ocean, and the study of geological processes and formations including sediments, minerals, fossils, continents, glaciers, and volcanism.

To build a career in geoscience you must have at least a master's degree in one of the geological sciences. The geosciences include sedimentology, stratigraphy, oceanography, mineralogy, volcanology, seismology, geochemistry, geomagnetism, and paleomagnetism. Some disciplines, such as paleontology and biological oceanography, include studying the ways in which life has influenced geological features, as in the creation of fossils and sediments. A geoscientist must have a background in geology and oceanography, and also in physics, chemistry, and mathematics.

Essential Gear

Geoscience = Computer Science! Computer skills are a necessity for all geoscientists. No matter what your field, you will be using computer tools for data analysis, mapping, modeling, seismic studies, and remote sensing. Satellites, especially those used in global positioning systems, have become basic tools of the trade. Brush up on your computer skills now, become familiar with applicable programs and applications, and always be open to learning new skills and new programs.

The geosciences are applied sciences. Most workers spend the majority of their time observing and measuring features, collecting data, analyzing samples, or seeking and studying deposits. A geoscientist should expect to be actively engaged in fieldwork, often at remote locations with primitive facilities. A prospective geoscientist must be able to enthusiastically cope with outdoor work, harsh weather, extreme conditions, and extended periods of time in the field. Good physical condition, endurance, appreciation of travel and outdoor living conditions, ability to get along well with others in a challenging environment, and a sense of humor are skills that may be as important on a day-to-day basis as facility in math and science.

The primary fields within geoscience are geology and geophysics. Geology focuses on the history and formation of geological and geobiological features, whereas geophysics includes in-depth chemical analysis of mineral and water deposits and the study of atmospherics, electrical activity, seismology, magnetism, and gravity. All geoscientists should have strong background knowledge of stratigraphy, topography, and cartography. The ability to use global positioning systems has recently become a key skill.

Although it is possible to find some entry-level positions with a bachelor's degree, most geoscience positions require a master's degree, with advanced research and faculty positions requiring a Ph.D. It is projected that a master's degree will become the minimum requirement for all entry-level geoscience positions in the very near future. A bachelor's degree in geology, oceanography, geography, astronomy, paleontology, physics, chemistry, biology, or engineering can provide a suitable foundation for advanced work in a specific geoscience. Coursework must include mathematics and computer science. Analytical thinking, spatial awareness, and written and interpersonal communication skills are also essential for the data-heavy, teamwork-oriented nature of research in this field. Due to the frequent travel required for fieldwork, fluency in more than one language is an asset.

University laboratory and research assistant positions and fieldwork internships are typical first-time jobs for those beginning down the geoscience path. Exceptional employment growth is currently being experienced in this field and is expected to continue. Most job openings are in private industries seeking to exploit high-value natural deposits, particularly of petroleum but also of minerals and aquifers. Conversely, the pollution of soil, air, and water, and the destruction of wetlands, coastlines, fisheries, and other ecosystems has led to an increased demand for researchers within some federal agencies and environmental protection organizations. Geoscientists such as seismologists are employed on construction and infrastructure projects and in facilities monitoring earthquake activity. The U.S. Geological Survey and state geological surveys have traditionally been the primary employers of geoscientists but openings have decreased in recent years due to budget cuts and an increase in the government's use of private contractors. However, the growth of demand within private industry (including independent contracting and consulting firms) and nongovernmental organizations has forestalled a reduction in available entry-level positions.

Job security varies between highly speculative businesses such as petroleum, coal, and mining interests and less cyclical areas of endeavor such as those concerned with engineering, safety, and research. The high investment in education required in this field is rewarded with high salaries, with 2006 median annual incomes averaging over $72,000 and mean entry-level salaries between $40,000 and $50,000. The roughly 2,600 geoscientists employed by the U.S. federal government in 2007 enjoyed average annual salaries of approximately $87,000 for geologists, $93,000 for oceanographers, and $100,600 for geophysicists.

You Are Here

Your journey to becoming a geoscientist can begin from more than one stepping-stone.

Are you new to the sciences? If you are new to the sciences, you will have to return to school to earn a bachelor's degree in geology or oceanography followed by a master's degree in a geoscientific specialty. Consider whether you are in a position to return to school full time or part time, and how much time, money, and effort you are able to invest in making this career change. You must not be intimidated by mathematics or computers, and be able and willing to learn new skills. An enthusiasm for fieldwork combined with good physical condition and the ability to work well with others are strong advantages.

Do you have a related degree? If you have a degree in the physical sciences, marine biology, engineering, mathematics, or computer science, you have already advanced several steps down your new career path, especially if your undergraduate career included coursework or fieldwork in geology, oceanography, or geophysics. Helpful courses include paleontology, atmospherics, geographical positioning systems, data analysis, structural geography, stratigraphy, mineralogy, chemistry, marine biology, oceanography, limnology, environmental and earth science, petrology, and physics.

Do you work in a related field? If you currently work in an applied science, engineering, or other career that is heavy in fieldwork, switching to geoscience may simply be a matter of seeking out a specialty and shoring up your academic credentials. Consider which geoscience you would like to specialize in. Contact federal and local geological surveys to investigate job openings and employment requirements. Create a résumé listing your academic background along with your employment experience and compare it to requirements for current job openings in your chosen field. Where are you already strong? Where do you lack academic, employment, or fieldwork experience? Having these "hard copies" to compare can make it easier to figure out the action you most need to take right now to continue down your chosen path. If you work in an applied science or engineering, seek out geoscience contacts and ask them

Navigating the Terrain

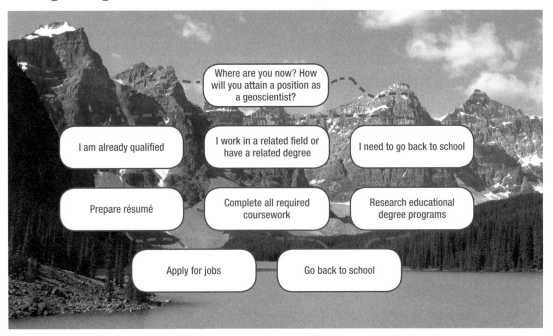

Where are you now? How will you attain a position as a geoscientist?

I am already qualified

I work in a related field or have a related degree

I need to go back to school

Prepare résumé

Complete all required coursework

Research educational degree programs

Apply for jobs

Go back to school

for advice. They may be able to point you to the most likely job openings and help you determine which academic steps are most critical to move quickly to your desired position from your current one.

Organizing Your Expedition

Before you set out, know where you are going.

Decide on a destination. Which element of geoscience interests you most? Do you prefer the heavy fieldwork and travel of geology, or the technical research and applied mathematics of geophysics? Do you live in earthquake country where there is a great need for seismologists, or would you prefer to spend your time traveling to remote locations for a geological survey? Does working as a geological scout for petroleum companies or mining interests appeal to you, or would you prefer to work for a nonprofit organization doing environmental remediation? Are you especially fascinated by the ocean and marine sedimentology, by fossils and paleontology, or by engineering earthquake-proof buildings

Notes from the Field
Jim Wilkinson
Engineering geologist
Cypress, California

What were you doing before you decided to become a geoscientist?

When I started in college, I never expected to become a scientist, let alone a geologist. I started out as a philosophy major, then a political science major. While in school, I was working for Nordstrom department store and was even considering a career in retail.

Why did you change your career?

I really had no idea what I wanted to do when I started college. I didn't think that science was what I wanted to do, even though I had always had an interest in science; I suppose I thought all the math and technical stuff would just be too hard.

I ended up taking a geology class for my science requirement; my instructor was incredibly dynamic and had amazing passion for the subject; this made learning much more fun. I was considering going into the military and began to think that a technical degree would be a valuable commodity. By the time I reached my senior year, I decided against the military as a career and was set on practicing geology.

How did you make the transition?

I had to complete a four-year degree in geological sciences. After I graduated, I started as a staff-level geologist doing all the grunt-work imaginable. As I gained more experience, my responsibilities grew. Eventually I was able to sit for the state license exam. After passing this exam, I was able to officially call myself a geologist. I worked in private

and transportation systems? Consider whether your dream job involves swinging a pick and sleeping in a tent, or sitting at a bank of computers and going home at the close of business hours. There is a huge variety to work with as far as choosing a geoscience discipline. Investment in school is heavy for this career, so it pays to be specific and commit yourself to the path you most desire. Look into all of the options and choose the one that is right for you.

industry for a number of years and then went to the State of California Environmental Protection Agency.

What are the keys to success in your career?

Like most careers, a good solid foundation in the basics is critical. Geology is really a culmination of chemistry, biology, physics, and geography; however, geology is also an art in the sense that experience and intuition factor heavily into the interpretation of geology. Since so much of what we are trying to understand as geologists is hidden, we rely on fragments of data to formulate hypotheses and theories. My background in philosophy taught me how to examine problems critically and how to formulate my ideas. My sales background helped me to communicate my ideas more effectively. I think much of whatever success I have achieved has come from a culmination of my life and work experience.

I would like to share that taking the required geology classes is only part of the education that prepares someone for success in their field. Whatever career someone decides to go into, they should receive a well-rounded education. Subjects you might not readily think offer value can really help later in life. Once while looking for a job, I met the owner of a small company I really wanted to work for. I met him at a professional society function and we started talking about different things, including travel and art. I had taken an art history class in school and was able to discuss the subject enough to get him to remember me. Later, I got an interview and was hired; I worked at the company for four years after that. I couldn't have gotten the job without my geology education and experience, but it was my ability to discuss other things with some degree of knowledge that set me apart from others who were interested in the same job.

Scout the terrain. Which schools offer applicable courses in your area? Which ones offer advanced degrees in your field, and what are the placement demographics for their graduates? Does the U.S. Geological Survey have offices, research facilities, and openings in your area? How about your state geological survey? Would you be willing to move to continue your education or for the right job? Are you open to travel for internships and fieldwork? Investigate local dominant industries and their need for someone with your proposed education and skill set. Mining, petroleum, and water interests, building contractor, architectural, and engineering firms, and agricultural or environmental organizations may all be fertile places to begin your career search. Investigate governmental organizations and their need for someone like you. Consider all areas where the skills you acquire might be applicable. While the U.S. Geological Survey is the most obvious, other agencies such as the Forest Service, Bureau of Land Management, and National Oceanic and Atmospheric Administration may also have employment opportunities for geoscientists.

Essential Gear

Writing Skills: Money, Please! Whether you go to work for a government agency, a college or university, or a consulting firm, writing skills will serve you well. If you work in private industry, marketing yourself and your company's services will be necessary to your job security. If you work for a government agency or academic institution, a key element of your employment will involve making sure that your funding continues. You will do this by designing research programs and writing grant proposals, and by presenting your research in such a way that those who funded it believe their investment to be a worthy expenditure. You must be able to convince investors that your program is important and interesting enough that they wish to give their money to you to make it happen. Effective proposals require clear and convincing writing by someone with excellent communication skills. Make sure that someone is you!

Find the path that's right for you. Consider all aspects of your new career path. Determine which geological science most appeals to you and target it specifically. Determine the level of education you need to accomplish, the type of job you want, and the possibilities for staying in your area to achieve them or moving to a new location. Consider which options are open and where you need to invest your time and energy. If you get seasick at the sight of a boat, perhaps oceanography is not the proper discipline for you. If you are a lifelong environmentalist, you may not wish to target that entry level position with the petroleum company, even though it would give you employment experience. If you can afford to switch careers and continue your education, you can also afford to be very specific about exactly what you need to accomplish to stay on course toward exactly the kind of job you want, without making unnecessary detours. Now is the time to determine what your plan should be and how to put it into action.

Go back to school. Carefully consider the level of schooling you already have and what additional level you need to attain. If you are new to the sciences, you will have to go back to school as an undergraduate. Geoscience encompasses a very large number of subjects. If you do not already have experience in these sciences, it may pay to spend some time exploring them to determine the area in which you wish to specialize. Enroll in courses at your local community college. This is a very affordable way to introduce yourself to a broad array of fields. Most community colleges offer a selection of geography, geology, and oceanography courses, as well as basic courses in geographical positioning systems, engineering, physics, mathematics, chemistry, and computer science. Explore now so that you can accurately and logically map out the next steps in your journey. Keep an eye out for relevant research assistant, fieldwork, and internship opportunities.

If you already have a bachelor's degree in the physical sciences, marine biology, engineering, mathematics, or computer science, you will have to earn a master's degree in a geoscientific field. Decide whether you need further undergraduate coursework or can move straight into an advanced degree program. See which programs are most appealing and applicable to you, investigate their application requirements, and apply. If you already have an advanced degree in the sciences, determine whether you already have the academic and employment credentials necessary to enter the geoscience job market. In addition to advanced education, some states require that certain geoscientists be licensed. Find out whether yours is one of them and what the requirements are by consulting your state licensing board.

Landmarks

If you are in your twenties . . . If you are currently an undergraduate, concentrate on geoscience and related courses. Declare a major in an applicable field or, if none is available at your current institution, transfer to a more appropriate college or university. Investigate research, fieldwork, and internship positions in your chosen field and related fields. If you already have a bachelor's degree in a related field, choose a master's program and, while you are doing so, work on acquiring basic experience. Volunteer positions with U.S. government agencies and environmental organizations are a great way to get your foot in the door while you are pursuing a degree.

If you are in your thirties or forties . . . If you do not already have a bachelor's degree in a related field, you will need undergraduate experience in the physical and geological sciences. As you pursue this, keep in mind that a master's degree is your minimum starting point for employment. Look into master's programs and complete any necessary undergraduate work with these programs in mind. If you already have a bachelor's degree in a related area, find master's degree programs in your chosen field and apply for enrollment. In the meantime, seek out related employment and volunteer positions.

If you are in your fifties . . . You should already have at least a bachelor's degree and experience in a related field. If you do, apply for master's programs. If you do not, be willing to carefully consider whether this is the right choice for you and, if so, to return to school full time. If you already have a master's degree in a related field, consider whether a doctorate will further your career goals, and begin your search for geoscience employment.

If you are over sixty . . . A master's degree with commensurate employment experience is preferable. If you already have the necessary academic and employment qualifications, use whatever contacts you have to seek out employment in your chosen field. If you do not, consider the schooling you will need, your employment prospects, and whether you are able and willing to return to school. If you are aiming for a career in applied geology, you must be in good health and excellent physical condition. If you are interested in geophysics, you must be adept at mathematics and computer skills.

Further Resources

The **U.S. Geological Survey** has traditionally been the largest and most well-known employer of geoscientists in the country. It has an extensive Web site filled with maps, research reports, and other publications, as well as job opportunities. http://www.usgs.gov

The **American Geological Institute** is an organization comprised of professional associations. Its goal is to promote the geosciences. It provides information on education, public policy, and research, as well as career opportunities. http://www.agiweb.org

The **American Association of Petroleum Geologists** provides information on educational options and career opportunities for those interested in petroleum geology, as well as information on research projects and conferences. http://www.aapg.org

Grant Writer

Grant Writer

Career Compasses

Get your bearings on what it takes to be a successful grant writer.

Communication Skills to write effective grant proposals that will gain funding for your project or organization (40%)

Organizational Skills to keep track of deadlines, funding needs and guidelines, and to follow up with funding agencies (30%)

Caring reflected in a thorough understanding of the projects you are supporting and commitment to their success (20%)

Ability to Manage Stress to achieve clear and effective communication while managing deadlines and dealing with financial matters (10%)

Destination: Grant Writer

If fund-raising or writing is your forte, you may have already composed the outline for a career in grant writing. Grant writers work for government agencies and research facilities, colleges and universities, and community, public, and nonprofit organizations. Anywhere where projects are in need of funding, someone must apply for grants. Large organizations engaged in continuous research or development projects may employ full-time grant writers. Smaller organizations may employ grant writers part time, on an hourly basis, or as independent contractors on a per-project basis. In some cases, grant writing is an element of the jobs of many people, rather than a distinct category of employment.

To be an effective grant writer you must be able to target appropriate funding agencies, write clear and convincing grant proposals, and have the organizational and communication skills necessary to follow up with prospective funding agencies as well as with ones that have granted funding. To do this, you must have a clear understanding of the projects for which you are seeking funding, and be able to communicate exactly how awards will be used.

A grant is an allotment of money awarded to an individual or an organization to fund a specific, defined goal. Unlike loans, grants are not paid back. However, all expenses paid for with grant money must be justified and the awardee must be able to prove that the funds served their intended purpose. In some cases, funds left over upon completion of a project must be returned to the granting agency.

The two main types of granting agency are federal and foundation. The federal government issues a variety of grants for a variety of purposes. Though the most well-known types of federal grants are those issued to individuals as financial aid to pay for college, federal grants are also awarded for educational and community development programs; environmental programs; scientific research programs; and public health, housing, and humanitarian efforts. Foundation grants are awarded by private foundations. These foundations can be strictly philanthropic or may be organizations based on furthering such causes as scientific knowledge, medical research, wilderness conservation, or environmental remediation. The foundations may be private or public; nonprofit or linked to a corporation, endowed trust, or political party; or secular or sectarian.

Essential Gear

Be Internet savvy! Grants are available from foundations with every imaginable background, guiding philosophy, and interest. The easiest way to find these foundations is online. Practice your Internet sleuthing skills, but make sure that you also have excellent Organizational Skills to process the information you will find, research skills to investigate the backgrounds and histories of organizations, and formal letter writing skills to effectively communicate with appropriate funding sources in a professional manner.

The primary role of the grant writer is to seek out and target appropriate funding agencies. The writer investigates federal and foundation grant programs, looking for ones whose goals most closely match the mission of the organization requesting the grant. Most of this research can now be done online but one must still carefully examine the background and goals of foundations and federal agencies as well as the stated purposes of grants before investing time and effort in appealing for funding. For example, if one were writing a proposal for the development of a new pharmaceutical product, it could prove embarrassing to target a foundation with a history of funding animal rights causes. To be a successful grant writer, you must know your audience as well as be intimately familiar with the goals of the organization hiring you to secure grants.

After appropriate funding agencies have been targeted, the next step is to write a grant proposal. A grant proposal is the document where you ask for money, explain why your project is valuable enough to deserve money, and give a detailed plan for exactly how grant money will be used. This includes presenting a budget as well as outlining the project's goals and how they will be achieved. You will be held to account afterwards for proving that the funding was used appropriately, so the goals must be clearly defined and realistic from the beginning. Most funding agencies have guidelines for which proposals they consider. These guidelines include deadlines for submission as well as requirements for cover letters, formatting, and number of pages, as well as for supplementary materials such as biographies of key parties and history of your organization.

A good grant writer researches the requirements and abides by them. A grant proposal must be clearly and professionally written with excellent grammar and spelling. You must be on the lookout for typos or incon-

Essential Gear

Make a commitment to writing well. Passion and dedication can be important in fund-raising, but they are only part of the story. The best project in the world will never be funded if its mission is not expressed clearly, concisely, and convincingly. Be sure that your writing has these qualities and is free from grammatical, spelling, punctuation, and typographical errors. Be able to write a formal letter of inquiry as well as a professional cover letter, and always remember to follow formatting instructions and deadlines. After all, if an organization cannot be trusted with proofreading and deadlines, why would anyone ever trust it with money?

sistencies, and willing to proofread and re-proofread until the proposal is perfect. Sometimes a small error spells the difference between being approved for a grant and being denied funding. The grant writer must be able to keep track of deadlines as well as to follow up on proposals after they have been submitted. It is wise to keep a detailed list of successful and unsuccessful proposals, as well as of the outcome of projects, so that one can learn which strategies are most effective.

Most research, development, and educational programs are funded by grants. Since these grants must be continually sought and renewed, grant writing is a consistent part of these programs. At one time many programs hired full-time, professional grant writers. As budgets are cut and funding becomes more scarce, fewer organizations have the funds or the inclination to do this. Many now rely on professional grant writers who work as independent contractors and are hired for specific projects, or require that researchers write their own grant proposals. In this sense, there has been a decline in the job market for grant writers. However, since the need still exists, and a professional writer who can write clearly, convincingly, and compellingly is vastly superior to an inexperienced writer who is approaching a grant proposal as an additional, unwelcome chore, there remains a relatively active demand for experienced, professional, and effective grant writers. Whether you aim to ultimately be hired as a full-time grant writer, decide to offer your services as an independent contractor, work part time, or as an administrative assistant with grant writing duties, you will need to apply your communication and marketing abilities to convincing potential employers of the necessity of your services as well as to securing grants.

You Are Here

You can turn the page to a grant writing career from several points.

Do you have a career in a related field? The two most important skill sets for a grant writer are writing and fund-raising. Do you already work as a professional writer? Your next step may be to put together a résumé and writing samples and begin targeting potential employers. Look for grant writing positions but be open to related positions such as copywriter, administrative or research assistant, and fund-raiser. There is a lot of crossover in many agencies between grant writing and other roles, so consider that the most direct path to your dream position may not be the most obvious one. Do you have professional or volunteer experience in fund-raising? If you can also write well, you are more than halfway there. Work on writing sample proposals, put together a résumé, seek out good references, and begin investigating employment opportunities.

Do you already have experience writing grant proposals? If you already have experience writing grant proposals and wish to gain a full-time position as a grant writer, your résumé, writing samples, and references are key. Use contacts you have already made to seek out advice and opportunities for employment. If you wish to head out on your own and begin an independent grant writing business, consider your next step. Marketing your business will be critical to your success and, at this time, that means having a Web site. Making certain that your Web site is easy to find and to navigate is especially important. If you do not have the skills to build one yourself, you will have to hire a Web designer. Research this process carefully to determine what you will realistically need to spend for the quality you desire. It may be less than you think, or than you have been led to believe. Depending on your area, you may need to obtain a business license. Investigate local ordinances governing small businesses and be sure to meet any legal requirements. Your local chamber of commerce may serve as a valuable resource.

Do you have a related degree? While there is no specific educational requirement for becoming a grant writer, certain degrees or coursework may help. A degree in English or communications, or in liberal arts from a school known for its emphasis on writing, can be especially helpful. You must be certain that your writing and proofreading skills are honed and of high quality before pursuing this career. There are a number of copywriting and grant proposal writing courses. Some of these are available for a fee through regular college programs or as community extension courses. Still others are provided free of charge by public or federal agencies. If you feel you have the drive, initiative, or experience to be a grant writer but are uncertain about your writing skills, one of these classes or related coursework at your local community college may be in order.

Navigating the Terrain

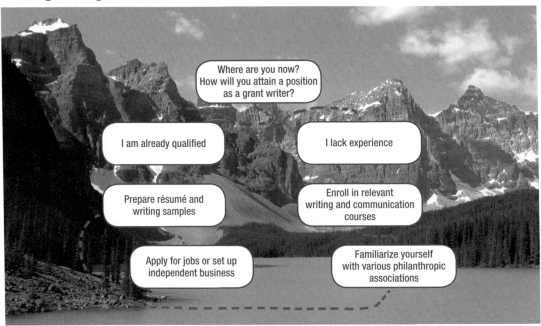

Where are you now?
How will you attain a position
as a grant writer?

I am already qualified

I lack experience

Prepare résumé and
writing samples

Enroll in relevant
writing and communication
courses

Apply for jobs or set up
independent business

Familiarize yourself
with various philanthropic
associations

Organizing Your Expedition

Before you set out, know where you are going.

Decide on a destination. What sort of employment situation would you prefer? Full-time grant writing positions may be few and far between and, as such, highly competitive. Investigate openings in your area. Educational institutions, public service associations, nonprofit organizations, and health care, science, and research facilities are all possibilities. You may find that available grant writing positions are part time, hourly, or per-project, or that grant writing is included as an element in the job description of a different position altogether. Decide whether you prefer having the specific job title, or are willing and able to work in a slightly different capacity that includes grant writing duties. If you are considering offering your services as an independent grant writer, research similar businesses on the Internet.

Scout the terrain. Investigate federal, public, nonprofit, and corporate employment options. Consider the types of organizations you would be willing to work for and the causes you would feel best about helping raise funds, then seek out positions in those areas. You may want to take some time to investigate funding agencies online. Just for fun, make up a project and pretend you are seeking grants. Which agencies would you approach? How would you draft your proposal? Do you really believe in your cause and did you communicate it convincingly? Was your proofreading effective? After reading your proposal, would you award it a grant? Enlist the help of friends to gain different perspectives on your approach.

Find the path that's right for you. If you lack confidence in your writing, go back to school. Depending on your current educational and employment background and the position you are seeking, a degree may not be necessary. A class or two in English, writing and composition, communications, technical writing, editing, or copywriting may be all that you need if you can back this up with excellent writing samples. See what is available at your local community college or through extension courses. Most colleges and universities offer noncredit extension courses in a variety of subjects to the general public, and you do not need to be enrolled in the school to take them. Grant writing courses are available through a variety of organizations and many can be completed online. Brush up on your skills and begin your hunt for the ideal job!

Landmarks

If you are in your twenties . . . Your first step is to ensure that you have excellent writing skills. If you are an undergraduate, take writing-related courses or apply to schools that have a reputation for being writing-heavy. Liberal arts programs can help you both perfect your writing skills and learn to present arguments convincingly from a wide variety of perspectives in a huge variety of subjects. Seek out organizations whose projects are funded by grants to gain on-the-job experience. Internships and volunteering may be valuable ways to make useful contacts as well as to gain experience.

Notes from the Field

Toni McCarty Rockis, Ph.D.
President/CEO, McCarty & Associates
Morris, Illinois

What were you doing before you decided to become a grant writer?

Before becoming a grant writer, I was a high school special education teacher.

Why did you change your career?

After teaching a few years, I decided to go back to school for an advanced degree. When I began my graduate studies, I mentored with an individual who wrote grants and also taught university classes. After learning how to write successful grant proposals, I decided to follow in her footsteps—to teach at the university and write proposals as part of my service to the community.

How did you make the transition?

My transition from teaching to grant writing was pretty simple because it was part of my transition to graduate school, and working with a mentor made it much easier to learn how to write successful grant proposals.

I now work with individuals who want to transition from their current careers into grant writing. Many of these individuals were in traditional nine-to-five careers, and they wanted to get into freelance grant writing so they could control their own work schedule and be their own boss, increase their income, and work from home. Many of them found that they could learn to write successful grant proposals while they were working in their nine-to-five job, and then slowly transition into full-time freelance grant writing as they picked up new clients.

What are the keys to success in your new career?

Grant writers are generally people who want to provide a service that contributes to society. Whether it's getting money for a new church

If you are in your thirties or forties . . . Seek out employment opportunities. Remember that grant writing itself may not be the only, or even the primary, job description. Consider your employment, educational, and volunteer experience to date and see where you may be able to apply these to your new career goals.

organ, updated technology for a local school district, or building a new park, grant writers want to help others better their communities.

If you decide to freelance, you should have an entrepreneurial spirit—this means having a positive attitude about your career, being highly motivated to become financially independent, and being able to multi-task. Of course, it goes without saying that you need to develop your writing skills. This can easily be done, simply by reviewing numerous winning grant proposals and picking up ideas to use in your own proposals.

Today, in the United States alone, there are more than 72,000 foundations that fund grants. These foundations issued grants totaling more than $42.9 billion in their last annual funding cycle (The Foundation Center, 2008). There are also 26 large federal agencies—like the U. S. Department of Education (USDOE)—that fund grants every year. Last year alone, the USDOE issued grant awards totaling more than $44.9 billion (USDOE, 2008). On top of this, state government agencies fund millions of dollars every year in grants.

Despite the large number of grants funded each year, there are very few good grant writers. This means that there's a lot of opportunity for anyone wanting to learn how to write successful grant proposals.

Generally speaking, beginning grant writers make anywhere from $25.00 to $50.00 an hour, while accomplished, experienced grant writers can make as much as $250.00 to $300.00 an hour or more. So, as a freelance grant writer, your salary will depend upon how much you want to work. Alternatively, you can always accept a nine-to-five grant writing job with a nonprofit community organization or school district. Your salary will then be dependent upon what the organization can pay you. My recommendation is this: Find a grant writing mentor, read as many successful grant proposals as you can get your hands on, and begin writing!

If you are in your fifties . . . The advice given for people in their thirties and forties applies to you as well. All experience writing or fund-raising will help you. Try to parlay past experience and contacts into opportunities for grant writing. If you worked as a registered nurse, for instance, your knowledge could help land you a job writing grants for medical research institutions.

If you are over sixty . . . Being able to navigate the Internet is now an essential component of all research and communication jobs. You must be confident in your ability to work online. If you need help in this area, most community extension programs have very basic computer courses designed to help older adults learn to operate common programs and navigate the Internet.

Further Resources

Wise Geek is a Web site devoted to answering questions about common subjects. Its section on grant writing is extensive and covers everything from how to target funding agencies and write grant proposals to finding grant writing courses.   http://www.wisegeek.com/s/grant-writing

The **U.S. Department of Health and Human Services** runs a Web site intended to list all available federal grants and their application guidelines.   http://www.grants.gov

The **Foundation Center** provides an online directory of philanthropic organizations that award grants. It also gives advice about fund-raising and nonprofit management. The site can be searched by geographical location and area of interest. Training courses are also available. http://foundationcenter.org

Health and Safety Technician

Health and Safety Technician

Career Compasses

Get your bearings on what it takes to be a successful health and safety technician.

Relevant Knowledge of legal regulations, hazards, and safety precautions (30%)

Organizational Skills to assess risks, calibrate equipment, take samples, and work in potentially hazardous environments (30%)

Communication Skills to effectively communicate safety needs and to manage situations that may become confrontational (30%)

Caring about hazards to human health and welfare (10%)

Destination: Health and Safety Technician

The role of a health and safety technician is to predict, prevent, and reduce accidents in the workplace. Health and safety technicians may work for government agencies enforcing regulations, for private industries or public institutions assessing and reducing risks, or for insurance companies investigating claims and inspecting clients. Health and safety investigators may be classified as technicians or specialists. The primary role of the technician is to collect data. Technicians take samples, test machinery, and investigate workplaces for compliance with safety standards and regulations. The primary role of a specialist is to analyze data. Specialists study the data collected by technicians and use it to create safety protocols and to improve safety standards and training programs.

Government health and safety technicians investigate a wide variety of workplaces for compliance with worker safety, public health, and environmental regulations. They may work for federal, state, or local agencies. Their job includes filing written reports with appropriate parties and may include training managers and workers in safety precautions or levying fines for the violation of safety regulations. Technicians working for public facilities (such as schools or hospitals) and for private industries inspect their companies' workplaces for safety hazards in order to prevent injury to employees or clients, destruction of equipment and property, threats to public health or the environment, and violation of legal requirements that could result in fines or work stoppages. These technicians and specialists are often also responsible for suggesting new safety measures and for implementing training programs for workers and management. The private technicians can be seen as a protective element that stands between the organization and government health and safety inspectors, making sure that the company remains in compliance and instituting harm-reduction measures where necessary.

Loss prevention specialists are health and safety workers hired by private insurance companies. They investigate private and public facilities to determine whether the safety standards in operation make them an acceptable insurance risk. These technicians and specialists also ensure compliance with basic regulations and suggest improvements. Since the insurance companies' interest is in collecting payments while maintaining as low a risk of financial loss as possible, they are highly motivated to ensure that the strictest accident-prevention measures are enforced and will often insist on additional safety precautions beyond those legally mandated and enforced. When an injury claim is made against a company by a worker or a client, a legal violation is reported; or a company is accused of an accident that affects public health, technicians will also be called upon to assess and investigate the circumstances surrounding the claim.

As people who are hired to investigate potentially hazardous conditions, health and safety technicians are frequently exposed to hazards. A health and safety technician can expect to take measurements and samples of everything from lead to radioactivity to biological disease agents. Technicians may find themselves measuring noise levels outside of an industrial production facility one day, and down a mineshaft testing air quality and structural supports the next. The technician's job includes testing potentially dangerous machinery and materials as well as the safety procedures in use, which may not always be adequate. Being a health and safety technician requires a strong emotional and physical constitution. You must be able and willing to place yourself potentially in harm's way to ensure that a situation, facility, or piece of equipment is safe for workers or the public. You must also be able and willing to recognize dangers and to take appropriate safety measures yourself.

A technician must be detail-oriented, well-versed in current safety regulations, and able to keep up with new ones. An excellent memory and careful attention is required to inspect facilities and work stations for proper safety equipment, appropriate use of equipment, and other compliance with safeguards and regulations. Confrontation must not intimidate you, since you will be in a position of authority that requires you make regulations known and take action to see that they are enforced. Such action may lead to disagreements with managers, owners of facilities, and workers themselves. You may be put in the role of "bad guy" by facilities and persons who

Essential Gear

Emergency? Health and safety technicians are on the way! The current focus of public attention on emergency preparedness has led to broader responsibilities and greater job opportunities for health and safety technicians. Greater public awareness of the need to prepare for disasters—with precautions such as earthquake safety and flood control measures, combined with a greater sensitivity toward the possibility of human-made disasters such as explosions, armed attacks, and the release of biological agents—has meant that health and safety technicians are becoming more highly valued within a broader array of businesses and facilities than ever before. The role of health and safety technicians in perceiving potential threats, preparing for disasters, and training others to prepare for emergencies, as well as their responsibility to do so, can be expected to grow in upcoming years.

are not in compliance, and it will be your responsibility to uphold the law and formal safety standards regardless of the ill-favor of the people with whom you are working. At the same time, a technician or specialist should have excellent communication and interpersonal skills to avoid or reduce such confrontation. After all, the best way to ensure that people effectively implement a regulation is to be perceived as their ally rather than their enemy, and safety standards are ultimately meant to protect the lives and health of human beings. A tendency to seek out conflict is just as incompatible with this job as a compulsion to avoid it.

Essential Gear

Certificates, certificates everywhere! With so many certificates, where does one begin? The first step is to understand what different certificates mean. *Professional certification* is formal recognition of your qualifications by a professional organization. It usually includes a specific amount of employment experience in your field combined with a certain level of formal education. It may also include continuing education on an annual or other basis, testing, character references, and a fee or dues. *Vocational certificates* are earned through an academic training program. They may be offered by a community college, four-year college or university, or vocational trade school. As opposed to a degree, a certificate program usually involves enrollment lasting one year or less and does not require general education coursework.

Educational requirements to become a health and safety technician are a minimum of an associate's degree in occupational health and safety, industrial hygiene, or a related field with appropriate work experience. Some employers also accept completion of a certificate program as fulfilling the educational requirement, especially if you have already worked in a related field. Becoming a specialist requires a bachelor's degree in occupational health and safety or industrial hygiene, or in a related field with valid work experience. A strong background in chemistry, biology, physics, mathematics, and English is recommended for both positions.

Continued growth is expected in the health and safety field, particularly as workers and the general public demand more effective safety precautions. Income varies between private and public employees and type of industry. As of 2006 most health and safety technicians and specialists were earning between $40,000 and $70,000 annually, with federal government salaries occupying the higher bracket, state governments the lowest, and private industry in between.

You Are Here

You can begin your journey to becoming a health and safety technician from a variety of locales.

Do you work in a related field? If you work in a related field, such as laboratory technology, the physical sciences, construction safety, health physics or another health care field, engineering, ergonomics, insurance adjustment, or any occupation dealing with safety, investigation, or law enforcement, you may have a head start on becoming a health and safety technician. Investigate the requirements of agencies who offer professional certification to health and safety technicians. Create a résumé with your new career in mind, and compare it to current job openings. If you need to enhance your education, look into programs at your local community college or vocational schools. Certificate programs may qualify you for some positions depending on your employment history, educational background, and employment goals.

Do you have a degree in the sciences? If you already have a degree in the sciences or engineering, your foot is in the door. Look into the requirements for degree programs in occupational health and safety or industrial hygiene. Decide which classes you still need to take, and enroll in an appropriate curriculum. You may wish to investigate professional certification or, if your academic background is already comprehensive in the sciences, vocational certificate programs. During this process keep in mind that any related work experience (such as interning as a laboratory assistant or volunteering with an organization that deals with health and safety, such as a hospital or fire department) may help you.

Are you new to the sciences? If you do not have an academic or employment background in the sciences you will need to go back to school. Enroll in an associate's degree program or higher in occupational health and safety or industrial hygiene. Important additional courses are chemistry, biology, physics, and mathematics. English and speech classes may help you develop your communication skills. During the course of your studies, be ready to take advantage of opportunities to work as a laboratory or research assistant, or in related internship and volunteer positions.

Navigating the Terrain

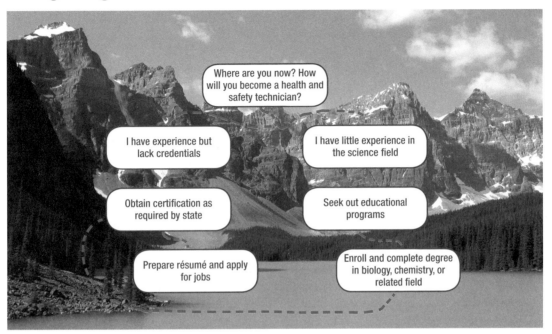

Where are you now? How will you become a health and safety technician?

I have experience but lack credentials

I have little experience in the science field

Obtain certification as required by state

Seek out educational programs

Prepare résumé and apply for jobs

Enroll and complete degree in biology, chemistry, or related field

Organizing Your Expedition

Before you set out, know where you are going.

Decide on a destination. What type of health and safety worker would you like to be? If your preference is for the nitty-gritty, hands-on work of sampling and inspection, a technician position may be right for you. If you love formulating plans and leading training programs, you may be aspiring to a specialist position. You will have to adjust your educational plan accordingly. Under what types of conditions do you prefer to work? Do you fantasize about the peripatetic life of a government investigator, traveling from place to place, measuring radioactivity in a nuclear power plant on a Monday and inspecting life preservers on a fishing boat by Tuesday? Or would you prefer to remain in a single facility, making sure that your employer is abiding by the law and that your fellow employees are consistently following safety protocol? Hospital, school, chemical manufacturer, insurance company, or government facility: the setting of each job makes the demands on the worker and the required skill set slightly different.

Stories from the Field

Patrick Callahan
Senior technician and manufacturing safety specialist
Rio Rancho, New Mexico

Sometimes a career in the sciences will lead to a different role entirely, such as community activist and whistleblower. Such was the case for Patrick Callahan. During his 18-year career as a manufacturing technician at Intel Corporation's Rio Rancho, New Mexico, microchip production plant, Callahan was exposed to many hazards—from full immersion in arsenic solution to chronic inhalation of vaporized isopropyl alcohol. Desiring to improve these conditions, Callahan transferred to a job as a health and safety technician for the company.

In this position Callahan uncovered numerous violations of safety procedures that put plant employees and contractors, as well as the public, at risk: unlabeled electrical wiring and improper operation of machines, absent exhaust vents and evacuation alarms, poorly-constructed equipment, and the release of toxic chemicals into the surrounding environment. He soon found that employment as a company's health and safety technician did not ensure the company would put safety recommendations into effect or correct violations. After repeatedly bringing numerous violations to the attention of management, and being repeatedly met with retaliation and threats of transfers to different departments,

Scout the terrain. If you need to return to school, see if appropriate degree programs are available in your area. Are you within commuting distance of the program you need, or will you have to move? Look at available job openings for health and safety technicians. Do they fit your preferences for workplace environment, duties, and level of travel, or do you need to look further afield?

Find the path that's right for you. Desired position, educational needs, and available job opportunities will each play a part in determining the path you take. Use your critical thinking skills to consider clearly and carefully what your personal strengths and weaknesses are, your workplace and lifestyle preferences, and your educational and financial needs, and embark on your journey. Consider all tools that may aid you, including professional certification, various vocational and degree pro-

Callahan blew the whistle. He took the next step—one that health and safety technicians are ethically bound to do—and filed formal complaints outside of the corporation. He gave his findings to the Federal Agency for Toxic Substances and Disease Registry, and alerted the surrounding community to the hazards in their midst.

In a 2007 interview, Callahan, who is recovering from chronic liver disease caused by his workplace chemical exposure, posed one of the dilemmas for industrial manufacturing workers and showed the need for interdisciplinary cooperation:

> *. . . the inventors are engineers, not industrial hygiene researchers. They invented machines and figured out 'if you mix this chemical and put it in a plasma field you can etch off metal.' Brilliant people came up with all the steps to make computer chips, but they never realized what the side-effects were to themselves or the workers . . . OSHA [Occupational Safety and Health Administration] and other agencies determine what the levels of any given chemical are that you can safely breathe for eight hours. There are other values for what is IDLH, 'immediately dangerous to life and health,' but what they never thought about is that those values are set for an eight-hour workday. At most computer chip factories you work 12 hours or more a day. Not only that, you're exposed to multiple chemicals during the course of a day. By being exposed to multiple chemicals in a longer than eight-hour workday, we were served a 'toxic cocktail.' There is no way to quantify what we were exposed to.*

grams, work experience you already have, and additional experience such as work-study programs, internships, and volunteer positions, and map your next step always keeping your goals in sight.

Landmarks

If you are in your twenties . . . The first step in becoming a health and safety technician is an appropriate degree. If you are currently an undergraduate, enroll in an occupational health and safety or industrial hygiene program. If such a major is not currently possible, concentrate in chemistry, physics, mathematics, and biology, and enroll in any available industrial or workplace health and safety courses. If you are not currently a student, seek out and enroll in a health and safety program.

If you are in your thirties or forties . . . If you are already qualified, consider professional certification and begin looking for appropriate job openings. If you are not, enroll in an occupational health and safety associate's degree program.

If you are in your fifties . . . You should have related work experience and a suitable educational background. If you have the educational background but lack work experience, look into current openings to get an idea of what your weaknesses may be and what steps you can take to strengthen your résumé. If you have work experience but lack academic credentials, see if there is a certification or continuing education program that will take your work experience into account, or if vocational training may be right for you.

If you are over sixty . . . You should already be qualified through employment experience and education. If you are not, consider whether becoming a full-time student is right for you. Also keep in mind the physical demands and hazards of a health and safety technician job, and whether you are both able and willing to meet those demands and take the associated risks.

Further Resources

The **National Institute of Occupational Safety and Health**, part of the U.S. Department of Health and Human Services' Center for Disease Control and Prevention, offers a huge selection of articles on occupational health and safety issues as well as career information. http://www.cdc.gov/niosh
The **American Industrial Hygiene Association** is a professional association that offers employment and career information including distance learning resources. http://www.aiha.org
The **Accreditation Board for Engineering and Technology** accredits educational programs in occupational health and safety, health physics, and industrial hygiene. Its Web site includes a feature to search for programs by institution, location, or program type. http://www.abet.org
The **Council on Certification of Health, Environmental, and Safety Technologists** offers examinations to be certified as a health and safety professional. http://www.cchest.org

Chemist and Materials Scientist

Chemist and Materials Scientist

Career Compasses

Get your bearing on what it takes to be a successful chemist or materials scientist.

Relevant Knowledge of chemistry (40%)

Mathematical Skills to perform operations, measurements, and calculations (30%)

Organizational Skills to process information correctly and efficiently in laboratory and office settings (20%)

Ability to Manage Stress while performing accurate and precise operations (10%)

Destination: Chemist and Materials Scientist

If you are fascinated by the composition and interaction of materials in your environment, you may have already mixed the basic elements to concoct a career as a chemist or materials scientist. Chemists study the structures, properties, and components of substances. Materials scientists specialize in classes of substance (such as metals, polymers, or ceramics) and use physics in their work as well as chemistry.

There are a huge number of specialties within the field of chemistry. Analytical chemists study the components of substances, organic chemists study carbon-based materials, inorganic chemists study non-carbon-based materials, physical chemists study substances' physical properties on the molecular and atomic levels, and theoretical chemists study the physical properties of matter itself and the natural laws which govern them. These broad fields are not the only disciplines within chemistry, however. Other specialties include macromolecular chemistry, which studies substances made up of macromolecules (such as proteins and polymers); medicinal chemistry, which studies the application of molecular compounds to medicine; cosmetic chemistry, which studies the application of compounds to cosmetic and hygiene products; biochemistry, which studies the chemical composition of living things; and materials chemistry, which focuses on the development of new materials for consumer products.

Essential Gear

Chemistry: Modeled by computers! Computer modeling uses a program within a single computer or a network of computers to graphically illustrate a process. The benefit is that a computer model can take abstract concepts governing a natural system and show the system working in the form of an animated event. A computer model essentially turns a large amount of abstract data, such as mathematical equations and chemical interactions, into a form that can be easily grasped by observers, where all variables may be considered simultaneously. This new technology requires that those entering the field of chemistry be familiar with computers and with the concepts and programs involved in computer modeling.

The chemistry and materials science field is currently undergoing a market shift. Most jobs in these fields have traditionally been with chemical manufacturing companies, but this is no longer the case as many of these companies cease operations or outsource projects to independent contracting firms. Some growth in employment opportunities is expected within these independent contracting firms. As environmental concerns become more central to public awareness, openings for chemists in regulatory, testing, public health, and conservation arenas are expected to grow. Industries involved in exploiting known energy resources as well as those in research and development for new sources are another area where chemists and materials scientists will find employment opportunities. Additionally, there is a consistent demand for qualified chemistry instructors at the secondary and post-secondary levels. The vast majority of openings for chemists and materials scientists, however, are within pharmaceutical and biotechnology companies.

The pharmaceutical and biotechnology industries are experiencing strong growth and this growth is expected to continue. Chemists and materials scientists are hired by these companies in research and development, testing, and quality control. Quality control tends to be the area that employs the greatest number of workers. Beginning chemists and materials scientists may also find entry-level openings with these companies as technicians, or even in such seemingly remote departments as marketing and sales.

Prior work experience and academic achievement requirements will vary based on the hiring company, particularly as all chemistry and materials science positions involve some amount of on-the-job training. The minimum level of schooling required for all positions is a bachelor's degree in chemistry or a related field such as physics, engineering, or environmental science, with a concentration in chemistry coursework. As these are competitive fields, the higher your formal education, the better your prospects for employment will be. Most research and development positions require a master's degree, and the highest positions require a doctorate.

Essential Gear

Biotechnology. While the term "biotechnology" may call to mind exotic entities like cyborgs and genetically engineered organisms, biotechnology is actually a very old and occasionally straightforward science. Biotechnology refers to any technology that uses organisms, living or dead, or their derivatives in its applications. The use of yeast to make bread or wine is biotechnology, and so is the use of bacterial and fungal cultures in pharmaceuticals, and the use of animal cells in the development of new medical treatments and devices. As you prepare to enter a career in chemistry, undergraduate courses in biotechnology may open your eyes to a broad range of biochemical applications—in daily life as well as within scientific research—that you have not yet imagined.

A chemist or materials scientist may work in a laboratory or an office, and most spend some time in each. Regular work hours are typical with the exception of specific research projects that require extended or unusual hours, and work on location, such as with an energy company or environmental organization. Earnings reflect the nature of this work as a highly skilled occupation, with median annual incomes of approximately $60,000 as of 2006, and starting annual incomes of around $40,000.

You Are Here

You can begin your journey to becoming a chemist or materials scientist from many different locales.

Do you work in a related field? A job as a laboratory technician or in any branch of the physical sciences may be good preparation for a career as a chemist or materials scientist. Related fields include physics, engineering, environmental science, and mathematics. If you have a degree in any of these fields, look at your actual coursework and determine where you still need credits. Employers tend to prefer as broad a background in chemistry as possible, so taking courses in a wide variety of chemistry fields—organic and inorganic chemistry, for example—plus other physical science and physics courses will help you. If you are interested in applying your chemistry knowledge to environmental science, take related environmental science courses such as atmospherics, oceanography, and limnology. If you are interested in biotechnology, courses in biotechnology, microbiology, and biology will be helpful. You should also have a strong background in mathematics including statistics, and be familiar with computer modeling. Computer skills are essential to employment in this field, as are written and verbal communication skills.

Do you have a degree in chemistry? If you already have a degree in chemistry, you are ready to begin your job search. If you are new to the sciences or have an unrelated degree, you will need to go back to school. An entry-level position as a chemist or materials scientist requires a bachelor's degree in chemistry or a closely related field with a great deal of chemistry coursework. If you are still in school or going back to school, take advantage of opportunities to work as a laboratory or research assistant. Internship, volunteer, and work-study experience in your chosen field now will help you get your foot in the door later, as will contacts you make with working chemists and materials scientists.

Do you have a related degree? If you have a degree in the physical sciences, engineering, environmental science, or mathematics, you may already have a solid academic background on which to put the finishing touches. Compare your transcripts and résumé to the requirements listed in current chemistry and materials science job offerings. Where are you already strong? Where do you need to return to school? Look into community college courses as well as programs offered by four-year colleges and universities. Also see what sort of enrollment options are available in your area. Some four-year universities allow enrollment in just a class or two for people who already have a degree or a strong academic background, but who still have a few gaps they need to fill to be competitive in the job market. A small number of schools offer degrees specifically in materials science. If you are interested in becoming a materials scientist as opposed to a chemist, and would like to earn a specific degree, check to see if any of these programs are available in your area. If you are new to the sciences you will have to enroll in a bachelor's degree program. The advice given in the above sections on choosing a program and specific coursework applies to you as well.

Organizing Your Expedition

Before you set out, know where you are going.

Decide on a destination. Consider your preferences as well as your experience and educational background carefully. The experience you have in your new career may vary widely depending on whether you are working for a federal agency, a conservation project, a pharmaceutical manufacturer, or a petrochemical company. Consider your personal interests as well as your academic strengths. Also consider your intended career trajectory. Are you interested in working in research and development, or eventually moving into a supervisory position, or is hands-on work in testing or quality control an end in itself for your dream job? Compare your actual interests and preferences, your educational and employment goals, and the openings available in the area where you live or where you wish to live, and allow all of these factors to guide you in finding your path.

Scout the terrain. Consider your next step carefully. Chances are that it involves returning to school. Take into account the amount of academic work you need to do as well as the time you are able and willing to invest in doing it. Are you ready and willing to return to school full-time, or is becoming a part-time student more your speed? Will your current employment accommodate this? Are appropriate educational programs available in your area, and do they include options for beginning

Navigating the Terrain

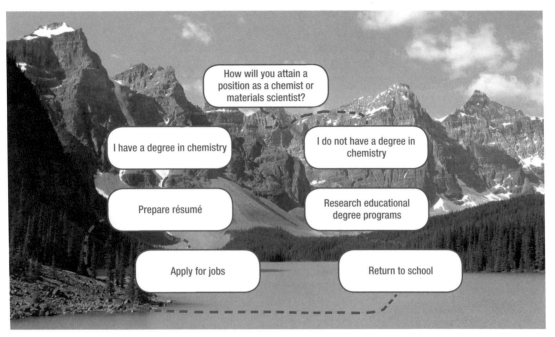

How will you attain a position as a chemist or materials scientist?

I have a degree in chemistry

I do not have a degree in chemistry

Prepare résumé

Research educational degree programs

Apply for jobs

Return to school

employment experience or financial aid? Consider elements outside of your specific field as well as you formulate your academic plan. Do your communication skills need work? Enroll in speech and writing classes. Are you familiar with computer modeling? If your last school experience was a decade ago or longer and your recent employment has not involved computers, you may need to take additional courses to develop your skills in this area. If your primary interest lies in biochemistry or biotechnology, be sure to take classes that relate to these fields as well, as change happens quickly and you will need the most current knowledge.

Find the path that's right for you. Keep your ideal employment situation in mind as you plot your next steps and return to school. If you have an associate's degree, put any applicable credits toward a bachelor's degree. If you already have a bachelor's degree, consider returning to school to earn a master's degree or a doctorate. Carefully consider the type of businesses you wish to work for and compare them to the jobs that are available in your area, as well as to your school's placement

Notes from the Field

Jonathan Reilly
Sensor manufacture engineer
Los Angeles, California

What were you doing before you decided to become a chemist?

I was working as a science temp doing bench work and document verifications for pharmaceutical companies in my area.

Why did you change your career?

It was the opportunity to work at a start-up company doing science every day. I was offered a chemist position, one of some authority and much more responsibility than I had previously been offered. After doing this for three years, my company was acquired by a much larger company and my department was phased out. I was given the opportunity to transition from being a Research Associate/Lab Manager to being a Process/Manufacturing Engineer. The product we make has both biological and electrochemical components and this was a good fit. It was also a very nice promotion.

How did you make the transition?

While my degree was in biochemistry, I had an extremely solid background in organic synthesis. I leveraged meticulous technique and prob-

record for graduates in your program. If the fit is not perfect where you are, consider whether you wish to move to find the ideal position. Use any available internship, volunteer, assistant, or work-study opportunities to gain relevant experience and clarify your path.

Landmarks

If you are in your twenties . . . If you are an undergraduate, declare a chemistry major and take classes that support your career goals. If such a major is not offered by your school, take steps to transfer to a more appropriate institution. If you are not currently a student, find institutions that offer your desired course of study, apply for admission, and enroll. Take advantage of opportunities to gain experience and make contacts in your field as you complete your studies.

lem-solving skills to transition to a role where I did organic synthesis and polymer chemistry. After my department was phased out, I put my problem-solving skills and biochemistry background to use troubleshooting, improving, and supporting a biochemical manufacturing line.

What are the keys to success in your new career?

Meticulous record-keeping in terms of laboratory notebooks is essential. Clear and open communication with everyone that you interact with is also critical. Learn how to effectively communicate with non-scientists as well as fellow scientists. While science requires incredible focus on the problem at hand, it is important to be able to step back and examine a problem or question at hand as a whole. Zoom out, rotate, look at something from a different angle. Often times complicated problems can be mitigated, if not solved outright, quickly, by examining the environment in which the problem exists. Look at the macro as well as the micro scale.

If you are reliable and liked personally by your coworkers and your supervisor(s), you will have a much easier and much less stressful career. While being very good at your job is important, no one wants to work with someone they do not like. It does not matter how good (or great) you are; if your boss doesn't like you, you won't be employed for long.

If you are in your thirties or forties . . . You will need a minimum of a bachelor's degree to continue down this career path. If you need to go back to school, consider all of the options in your area. If you already have a related bachelor's degree, your next step may be supplemental study at a community college. If you do not have a bachelor's degree, or have one in an unrelated field, your next step will be to investigate the options at four-year colleges and universities, perhaps while enrolling in introductory chemistry and related courses at a community college.

If you are in your fifties . . . You should either have career experience in a related field, a related degree, or the ability return to school full-time. The advice to people in their thirties and forties applies to you as well.

If you are over sixty . . . Ideally you already have related professional and academic experience. If not, consider whether you are able and willing to enroll in a full-time academic program. You are unlikely to encounter a great deal of age-related discrimination as a chemist or materials scientist, but guard against it to the best of your abilities by making sure you have the most up-to-date knowledge, including computer skills.

Further Resources

The **Office of Personnel Management of the U.S. Federal Government** provides the ability to search for government job openings in every possible field, worldwide, at its Web site. It also offers information on hiring processes and resources for veterans. http://www.usajobs.opm.gov

The **American Chemical Society** offers a huge database of research publications related to chemistry and materials science, as well as information regarding educational programs and career opportunities. http://portal.acs.org/portal/acs/corg/content

The **U.S. Department of Energy's Argonne National Laboratory** hosts a database of publications specific to materials science. http://www.msd.anl.gov

Science Teacher

Science Teacher

Career Compasses

Get your bearings on what it takes to be a successful science teacher.

Relevant Knowledge to teach science to students (40%)

Caring and patience to provide guidance and understanding to students (30%)

Communication Skills to convey lessons and concepts (20%)

Ability to Manage Stress while interacting with children or older students, parents, other teachers, and school administrators (10%)

Destination: Science Teacher

If you have patience, excellent social skills, and ingenuity you could be on the path to becoming a science teacher. Science teachers may teach at any grade level from elementary school through graduate courses, but most teach in the middle and high school grades, while a smaller but still significant number teach at the undergraduate level. As the second most in-demand category of teachers (after mathematics), science teachers have been protected from recent economic impacts to a greater extent than those in most other subjects.

There are similarities among teaching options, and several differences. One similarity is that you must have a formal postsecondary education that includes some type of proof that you are qualified to teach in your subject area. The differences depend on the type of school you target as your future employer. Science teachers are employed by public middle and high schools, private schools, online home schooling services, charter and magnet schools, tutoring services, community colleges, vocational schools, and four-year public and private colleges and universities. The credential requirements will depend on the hiring institution.

All primary and secondary public school teaching positions require at least a bachelor's degree. While some schools require a degree in education, most require a degree in the subject you wish to teach combined with licensure or certification. Prerequisites for licensing vary by state. All public schools require licensure. Private schools and tutoring services do not necessarily require licensure but they often require testing in your discipline. To teach science at most colleges and universities you will be required to have at least a master's degree, and many require a doctorate. The more competitive the school's program, the more likely it is to require the most advanced degree.

To teach science at the secondary level (grades 7–12) in a public school, you must be licensed in your subject area. The science subjects most commonly taught in middle and high schools are biology, chemistry, physics and physical science, and earth and environmental science. State licensing guidelines typically include tests for general competency as well as subject proficiency. Most states also require that prospective teachers complete a certain number of credits of college coursework in a specific set of subjects beyond the ones they are planning to teach. Completion of a teacher-training program with a certain number of hours of student-teaching is also typically required. In addition, many states require continuing education to maintain licensure. You will need to check with your state board of education to determine requirements. A few states have even stricter requirements, such as demonstrated classroom competence or enrollment in a master's degree program in education within a certain period of time after being hired. Some states allow transfer of out-of-state licenses, but be sure to find out which rules apply in your target area before deciding you "have license, will travel."

Despite the standard requirements, if you did not major in education or complete a prescribed set of general education courses while you were earning your degree, do not fear! Teacher shortages, particularly in mathematics and the sciences, have led a large number of states to set up alternative programs meant to facilitate the entry of career changers and recent college graduates into hard-to-fill teaching positions. The most famous of these alternative teacher-training programs is Teach for America, a division of the national community service organization AmeriCorps. This program typically enlists recent college graduates with the promise of student loan forbearance and, in some cases, cancellation. Application is also open to other professionals who have completed a bachelor's degree. Many states have instituted similar programs where those without a degree in education, or who have not completed teacher-training classes, may be granted a provisional license and be hired to work under the guidance of experienced, licensed teachers. Some of these programs involve additional college coursework leading to a master's degree, others require general education credits equivalent to those taken in a traditional teacher-training program, and still others grant emergency licenses to individuals in difficult-to-fill subject areas (math and science) without requiring any additional college coursework. Again, you must check with your state board of education and local school districts to see which options are in effect in your area.

Essential Gear

Which school is which? *Public schools* are schools administered by the state and operated through public funds. *Private schools* are administered by a wide array of sources, including religious, military, and private for-profit and nonprofit organizations. *Charter schools* are public schools operated at least in part by public funds but in accordance with a private charter, which sets each school's individual standards for admission, teacher credentials, and student performance. *Magnet schools* are public schools with specialized curricula (such as a "school for the sciences" or "school of art and music"), which accept talented and motivated students from a single district or several adjacent districts. *Tutoring services* and *portfolio schools* are private, part-time schools that have specific curricula such as science and math, reading, standardized test preparation, or art and design. *Home-schooling* services are virtual schools, which exist entirely online and are meant to replace traditional public and private schooling.

Teaching at a private school may not require the same education and licensure as teaching at a public school. It will pay to investigate job listings for private school teachers in your area, or contact the schools themselves for specific guidelines. Most private schools have Web sites that include information regarding job openings and hiring practices. Almost all require at least a bachelor's degree in your subject, but they may or may not require additional credentials such as general education credits or testing. There is wide variation in requirements within private schools.

Another option is part-time teaching, whether for a tutoring service or as a substitute teacher. Like private schools, tutoring services set their own standards for hiring. Most do not require licensure but almost all require at least a bachelor's degree and many prefer a master's degree. Most require testing in your subject as well as demonstration of classroom competence. With greatly increased national standardized testing requirements, the tutoring services industry is flourishing, especially in upper-income, urban areas. Most tutoring services provide part-time work to teachers at relatively high hourly wages, in settings that vary from one-on-one instruction to full classrooms of students. Tutors who are fluent in more than one language are particularly in demand. Requirements to become a substitute teacher vary by state but are often less stringent than to become a full-time teacher.

Though it is a cliché that teaching is a low-paying profession, annual income varies quite markedly by region, school, and subject. As of 2006, the majority of primary and secondary school teachers earned between $28,000 and $48,000 annually, while most postsecondary earnings were in the $39,000 to $90,000 range. Schools usually pay by salary, whereas tutoring services generally pay wages averaging $30 per hour.

You Are Here

You can begin your journey to becoming a science teacher from several different locales.

Do you have experience teaching? If you already have experience teaching, and know that it is a job you enjoy and at which you excel, you are well on your way. Teaching experience may come from outside the classroom, such as through leadership training, camp counseling, volunteer activities, peer education, coaching, and parenting, as well as from traditional classroom experience. The most critical elements in becoming a successful teacher are empathy, the ability to relate well with those you are teaching, and a talent for sharing your knowledge of a subject so that it is easily understandable. You must be able to engage the interest of your pupils and ease them through rough patches to a complete grasp of fundamentals while encouraging their critical thinking skills and motivating them to explore subjects further on their own.

Do you have experience in the sciences? If you already have a degree in the sciences you are more than halfway to your new career. Investigate the openings for science teacher positions in your area and then consider the requirements for each. Your options may vary from a path of least resistance where you simply test to become a tutor, to entering graduate school for a master's degree in education. Contact your state board of education for license requirements if you are interested in working at a public school, and see what expedited credential programs may be available to you. If your area is experiencing a shortage of science teachers, you may have options that allow you to begin work immediately. Look into programs such as Teach for America, traditional teacher training, and local provisional and emergency licensing, and decide which is right for you.

Are you new to science and teaching? If you have neither teaching experience nor a degree in the sciences, you will need to return to school. The choice that will give you the broadest range of employment options is to major in your subject area while also completing a traditional teacher training program. Look into college and university programs and apply to the ones you believe best suit you. Meanwhile, consider temporary or part-time employment and volunteer opportunities that will give you valuable teaching experience, such as youth programs or peer tutoring. As you enroll in college courses, keep state requirements as well as an idea of the types of schools in which you wish to work in mind. As you are "starting from scratch," however, it will pay to make yourself employable in as broad a range of institutions as possible.

Navigating the Terrain

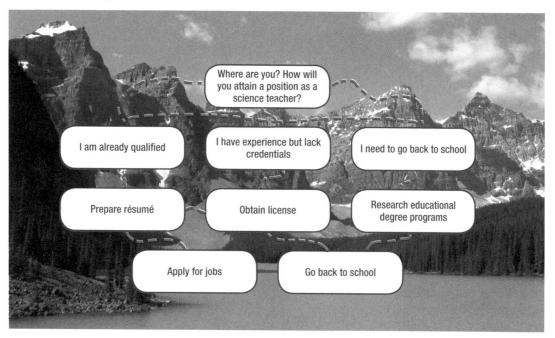

Organizing Your Expedition

Before you set out, know where you are going.

Decide on a destination. Even within the categories of public and private, secondary and college, there are huge variations between schools. Public schools include the single high school serving a sparsely populated rural district, as well as huge urban schools with thousands of students in each grade. They also range from under-funded, historically low-performing schools in desperate need of motivated and qualified teachers to small charter and magnet schools with ample funding and high levels of parent and community participation. Private schools have a similar, if not greater, range of variability, from conservative religious schools to socially progressive institutions with highly specialized philosophies of education, such as the Waldorf and Montessori schools. Tutoring services and substitute teaching positions also vary, and at the

Notes from the Field

Efrain Schunior
Charter school primary education teacher, grades 5-8
Los Angeles, California

What were you doing before you decided to become a science teacher?

I have done many things in my life. Most recently I completed graduate school and worked as a human resources manager for a large, upscale cinema in Hollywood.

Why did you change your career?

I decided to switch to teaching because I saw the impact I could make. The job became available and I jumped at the opportunity. After the first year, I knew it was the right path.

How did you make the transition?

It was difficult at first, trying to make the transition, understanding everything that was necessary to be effective and do the best for the

post-secondary level there can be vast differences between teaching at a community college, a private four-year college, a career college, or a large research university.

Scout the terrain. What positions are available in your area? Are you currently qualified to pursue them or ready to gain the appropriate credentials? Carefully consider all possibilities, from tutoring services through college instructor, and determine which ones best fit your personality and abilities. The options available to you will vary widely based on your geographic location. If you are in a rural district, science teacher positions may be limited to a very few, and mostly filled, tenured positions. If you are in a suburban area, private schools and tutoring services may be very common. If you are in an urban area, you may have the full range of teaching options along with a full range of individual variables to consider, from school violence to budget cuts and teacher firings. If the types of positions you wish to fill are unavailable in your area, are you willing to move? If so, what are the licensing requirements in your new area?

children but as I kept my ears open and actively sought guidance from the older, more experienced teachers, I slowly realized that I was becoming a better teacher.

What are the keys to success in your new career?

As a teacher, it's hard to remember that you are allowed to not know something. My motto is, "It's not about always having all the answers but about not being afraid to find out the answers." You don't have to know everything, you just have to be willing to keep discovering. Teaching is a very difficult career. It is a profession, remember that. If you approach it as a nine-to-five job, you will not be successful. You will always be facing budget cuts and others who aren't willing to help you. You'll always face tough administration and strange policies that feel like a bunch of red tape. As long as it burns inside of you, you'll be fine. Find a way to stay passionate about it and all the other extra stuff won't seem so bad.

Find the path that's right for you. Keep an open mind, use the Internet to help you find institutions that are looking for teachers, and be very honest with yourself about your desires, goals, and abilities. Finding the right career path will require an honest assessment of your options compared to your interests and abilities. Some people shine most brightly in a crowded public high school, where they become valued teachers who make all the difference in the lives of under-privileged youth. Others do better teaching adult learners at a community college, or private middle school students in a small, intimate, and well-funded setting. As a teacher, you are going to have an enormous impact on the lives and academic success of your students. Be honest with yourself regarding your interests and abilities and seek out the positions where your work will fuel the greatest good.

Landmarks

If you are in your twenties . . . If you are an undergraduate or a graduate student, enroll in a teacher-training program. If you are already enrolled in a teacher-training program, be sure to also take as many science courses as possible. If you are a recent graduate, contact programs designed to facilitate your entry into a teaching career.

Essential Gear

No child left behind? Passed into law in 2002, this act requires that every primary and secondary public school administer annual standardized tests to students, and that performance on these tests improve annually. This has been met with great disapproval by many educators, who claim that it has changed the emphasis within schools from producing well-rounded, educated, open-minded students to producing higher test scores at any cost. Effects have included more standardization within school curricula, which has meant far less freedom for teachers regarding what they teach and how they teach it. In many districts, particularly those in poor urban areas, it has also meant a loss of funding as teachers fight to increase test scores against facilities that are unfit, supplies that are inadequate, social situations where students are already at a disadvantage, and other sub-optimal conditions. Loss of funding has led to increased teacher layoffs and decreased hiring. Anyone entering the teaching profession at this time may have to grapple with these difficulties. So far, instructors working in science and mathematics have been largely protected from firings, but not from standardization of curricula.

If you are in your thirties or forties . . . If you already have a degree in the sciences, contact your state board of education to determine licensing requirements. Seek out programs designed to help you begin teaching while you earn your license. If you already have experience teaching but are new to the sciences, find out what the requirements are to become a science teacher in your state or at your preferred institutions, and return to school to fulfill those requirements.

If you are in your fifties . . . If you have not yet attended college, or have a degree in a subject unrelated to education or the sciences, return to school, preferably at an institution with teacher training and science programs that are both strong.

If you are over sixty . . . The advice given above applies to you as well. If you are new to the sciences and teaching, you will have to return to school for a science major and teacher training. Ask yourself if you are truly prepared to make this commitment at this stage of your life, or if you would prefer to teach in a voluntary capacity.

Further Resources

The **National Council for Accreditation of Teacher Education** provides a list of accredited teacher training programs by state. http://www.ncate.org

The **National Center for Alternative Certification** provides information about non-traditional routes to earning teaching credentials. http://www.teach-now.org

Preparing Future Faculty is a program run by the Council of Graduate Schools to give future postsecondary teachers experience working at diverse institutions under the guidance of experienced faculty mentors. Information and publications are available. http://www.preparing-faculty.org.

The **American Federation of Teachers** provides a great deal of information on all subjects related to teaching from the union's perspective. http://www.aft.org

AmeriCorps' **Teach for America** program provides teachers to low-income and struggling public schools by recruiting prospective instructors who have not completed a traditional teacher-training program. http://www.teachforamerica.org

Environmental Scientist

Environmental Scientist

Career Compasses

Get your bearings on what it takes to be a successful environmental scientist.

Relevant Knowledge of the physical, earth, and life sciences (40%)

Communication Skills to make data and information understandable to others (30%)

Caring and passion for work involving living things and their habitats (20%)

Ability to Manage Stress in challenging environments during fieldwork as well as during the reporting phase of projects (10%)

Destination: Environmental Scientist

Environmental scientists draw on a wide base of knowledge from all of the physical and life science disciplines to study the earth, the interplay of life and ecosystems, and environmental impacts caused by human activity or geological phenomena. Environmental science is an interdisciplinary field that includes ecology (the study of how life interacts with its environment), hydrology, biology, geology and earth science, chemistry, physics, and atmospheric science. Environmental scientists may also draw on oceanography, marine biology, zoology and animal science, botany, and forestry.

A broad background in these sciences is excellent preparation for a career as an environmental scientist. Many colleges and universities offer a degree in environmental science itself, though environmental scientists often have degrees in any of the life, physical, or earth sciences combined with coursework in many others and fieldwork experience. While the options for undergraduate majors are many, environmental science as a career requires advanced education. The minimum requirement for entry level positions is a bachelor's degree, while most positions and opportunities for advancement require a master's degree. A doctorate is required for almost all teaching and research positions. It is expected that educational requirements in this field will become stronger in the years to come with very few, if any, positions open to candidates with bachelor's degrees only.

Essential Gear

Global Positioning System. Since its creation in 1995, the GPS has become the most widely used satellite-based navigation system in the world. GPS transmitters "ping" the GPS satellite array. They determine the user's position by timing the signals sent between unit and multiple (usually more than four) satellites. The system was created by and is owned and operated by the U.S. Department of Defense but may be used by anyone free of charge. Its use has become a mainstay of all environmental work and of most computerized navigation systems.

The largest employer of environmental scientists is the government at both the federal and state levels. Other employers are consulting and contracting firms, natural resource extraction companies, infrastructure contracting firms, environmental protection and remediation organizations, and research universities. Most environmental scientists' work consists of performing environmental impact studies and natural hazard assessment, while some work in the field of oil, gas, aquifer, and other natural resource exploration, and others work on environmental remediation and restoration projects and habitat conservation.

The environment has experienced a large number of disastrous impacts as the result of human activities within the past three centuries. These have included the loss of entire ecosystems and species, and enormous damage to human lives and to nature-based industries. Disasters with human and natural components are capturing worldwide attention, such as the breached levees, flooding, mudslides, and tremendous loss of lives and property that have followed hurricanes and other storms in recent years. An ever-growing number of densely populated areas are at the mercy of rising sea levels, while fisheries are collapsing, forests and cropland are being turned to desert, and the threat of nuclear disaster once again looms imminent. The list of outrages and threats seems endless. Meanwhile, public awareness, concern, and education regarding these impacts have been steadily growing, leading to pressure for preservation and remediation. An immediate effect of this has been the growth of environmental science as a discipline, and the increased number of jobs available for environmental scientists. Career opportunities are expected to continue to grow faster than the average for science professions.

The majority of environmental scientists spend at least part of their time conducting fieldwork. This includes extended periods of living close to the land, studying particular systems or species, and taking samples and collecting data, almost always as part of a team living in close quarters. Outdoor work in extreme weather, heavy physical labor, and exposure to wildlife from bugs to bears are involved, as are frequent travel and relocation. Work in the field requires that you be sturdy and of good humor. You must also be in excellent physical and emotional condition, and able to work well with others in demanding circumstances. If you are committed to making a real, physical impact on protecting and preserving ecosystems, you will probably find an environmental science career very rewarding.

The other side of the environmental science equation is office work. After you have collected your data and studied your subjects or your samples, you will have to communicate your findings clearly and efficiently to the people paying for your project. This involves writing reports and, occasionally, scientific papers and journal articles. In order to secure funding, grant writing is also often necessary. Excellent written and verbal communication skills are essential. For some projects, laboratory work is involved. In each case, hours can be long and there is often little division between "work" and "home."

In many cases, especially if you have only completed a bachelor's degree, employment is on a per-project basis, meaning that after one project is completed, you will have to find a new employer. This can be challenging and involve a certain amount of stress. If you require consistent employment to feel secure and successful, your best bet is to earn a master's degree or higher and to apply for a position with a federal or state geological survey or other government agency based in a region where you wish to live.

Though the reported average annual earnings for environmental scientists were listed as $56,000 for salaried employees and $38,000 for entry level positions requiring a bachelor's degree as of 2006, earnings vary widely. They depend on many factors, including type of project, employer, and duration of employment. Some jobs pay only a stipend to cover living and travel expenses. With the lack of division between working hours and time off involved in fieldwork, the amount that even higher-paying positions provide often turns out to be very little when compared to the time invested. Thus environmental science is a field that requires true passion and commitment beyond the desire for a paycheck.

You Are Here

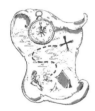

You can begin your journey to becoming an environmental scientist from many different locales.

Do you work in a related field? If you already work in a physical, earth, or life science, environmental conservation and remediation, forestry, or data collection and analysis, or have experience as a technician, laboratory or research assistant, or fieldworker, you may already have much of the experience and background necessary to become a working environmental scientist. Investigate employment options. If you need to supplement or complete your education, seek out schools with environmental science majors. If you are not already familiar with data analysis, computer modeling, global positioning systems, geographic information systems, or environmental management, law, and ethics, be sure to take courses that address these areas. Formal education in as broad an array of related fields as possible can only help you on your new career path, so keep an open mind and stay on the lookout for opportunities to learn new subjects or to approach familiar ones from different perspectives.

Do you have a related degree? If you already have a degree in earth science or geology, biology or another life science, ecology, chemistry, physics or geophysics, forestry, zoology or animal science, oceanography, hydrology, or atmospheric science, you may already have the basic background for an entry level position in environmental science. Seek these positions out while you also seek out and enroll in a master's degree program. Many of the positions available will be per-project and on location performing fieldwork.

Do you love the outdoors? Environmental science involves a greater degree of outdoor work than most other disciplines. If you feel the call of nature summoning you to this career, you are already most of the way there. Now you simply need to shore up your educational credentials and find relevant employment. Keep your eyes open for opportunities to gain necessary experience, including laboratory and research assistant positions, internships, and volunteer positions.

Navigating the Terrain

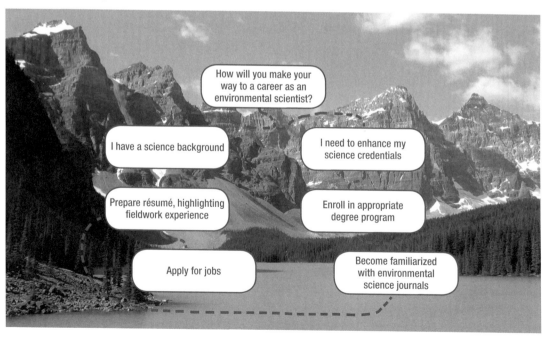

How will you make your way to a career as an environmental scientist?

I have a science background

I need to enhance my science credentials

Prepare résumé, highlighting fieldwork experience

Enroll in appropriate degree program

Apply for jobs

Become familiarized with environmental science journals

Notes from the Field
Nathan Libal
Wildlife researcher
Starkville, Mississippi/Whitehorse, Yukon Territory

What were you doing before you decided to become an environmental scientist?

Before choosing this career path, I was working at an industrial woodworking company. At the time, I had recently graduated from high school and was unsure of what I wanted to accomplish in my life.

Why did you change your career?

After working at the woodworking company for several months, I was sure that I didn't want to do that forever and I knew I wanted to continue my education. It took some time to sort everything out but I came to realize that what I wanted to accomplish in life was doing something I loved to do so that my job felt more like recreation than work. My interests have always revolved around the outdoors and conservation issues, so the logical choice was to go back to school and earn an environmental sciences degree.

How did you make the transition?

The first step was to get into a reputable environmental sciences program. A big part of getting a successful job in this field is being able to prove that you have had an extensive and varied education covering many environmental issues. I also volunteered for local environmental programs while at school. This included a variety of projects including invasive species removal, species inventories, and environmental experiments. Finally, I made an effort to network with other people in the field. I am not by nature a very outgoing person, but this is very important to do. The environmental field is a close-knit community and you quickly find out that people know each other, even if they work in distant places. Networking helped me to find job openings that I otherwise would never have known about, and has come in handy in several interviews.

What are the keys to success in your new career?

Today, the environmental field is extremely competitive and so it is important to keep several things in mind if you are considering this as a career. First, you have to attain the experience and knowledge that will set you apart in an interview. To get the right mixture of education, attend a university with a well-known environmental program. These programs are taught by some of the leaders in the environmental field and will cover a wide array of conservation/environmental topics. Having coursework that covers many topics is very helpful later on, as it makes you competitive in many different fields.

To improve your practical experience, volunteer during your school years. Employers like to see that you really care about environmental topics, and the experience you get can be just as significant as paid positions.

During the summers between semesters, do your best to get practical work experience in the field. The easiest way to do this is to approach professors and graduate students about their research projects and ask if they are hiring seasonal technicians. You can also search for technician positions online through several databases such as the Texas A&M University Wildlife Job Board or the Society for Conservation Biology Job Board. These positions are much more competitive, but it is worth a look. Another organization is the Student Conservation Association (SCA). This group has a database of seasonal positions that are only offered to students. While they do not pay a salary, the SCA does provide transportation reimbursement to get you to and from your position as well as a small living stipend. Depending on how long the position lasts, you also can become eligible for an AmeriCorps Scholarship that can be used towards your educational expenses.

Given how competitive the field is, you should consider getting an advanced degree. There is a huge pool of bachelor's-level employees right now. This makes it very difficult to get a full-time job, and also drives down the salaries of the jobs that are available. In order to make your career a financially feasible one, an advanced degree may be your best option to be more competitive in the job market and to make a reasonable wage.

From my own experiences, I do have a couple pearls of wisdom to share. The first is to sit back and make sure the environmental sciences field is really for you before embarking on this career path. It is not an easy one, and you have to be passionate about the environment to be successful. Jobs usually pay very little and require an enormous amount of dedication and commitment. Many of the positions I've held have paid

(continued on page 86)

Notes from the Field

(continued from page 85)
hardly enough to get by, have required 12 or more hours of work a day, and have been both physically dangerous and mentally taxing. This probably doesn't sound very appealing, but the flip side is that I've had the opportunity to work in some of the most beautiful places in the world and have helped make a difference in conserving our natural resources.

The other bit of advice I have is not to get discouraged. Many of the positions you will apply for will have dozens of other applicants just as qualified as you are. Inevitably, you will be turned down many times. Do not take this as a personal slight or as evidence that you are not good enough to get a job. You have to stay positive and keep applying. Determination is the greatest asset you can have when trying to break into this field.

Organizing Your Expedition

Before you set out, know where you are going.

Decide on a destination. Most jobs involve research and reports, whether on expected effects of a proposed project, on the potential for natural or human-made disasters, or on impacts that specific wildlife populations or ecosystems are already experiencing. The nature of the work is very similar across the board but the applications may be quite different based on whether you are working for a government agency, an environmental organization, a research university, a natural resources extraction company, a contracting firm, or a consulting business. Even within a certain category, such as the federal government, the use your work is put to may vary widely based on whether you are working for the Bureau of Land Management, the Forest Service, or the Department of Defense. Consider where and for whom you wish to work as well as subjects in which you wish to concentrate. If jobs are not available with the types of organizations you wish to work for in your area, relocate or consider your options for relocating while you return to school.

Scout the terrain. A great deal of travel or frequent moves are a requirement for most environmental science jobs. Whether or not this appeals to you will be a large factor in determining the positions you seek out. If it does, in what areas and under what conditions are you willing and able to work? If it does not, what positions are available in your area? If you need to return to school, your best options may include relocating right away. Most bachelor's and master's courses require fieldwork, and their programs as well as internship opportunities are often located far from the school itself. Be very clear about your interests and capabilities, and seek out educational programs and positions that capitalize on your strengths.

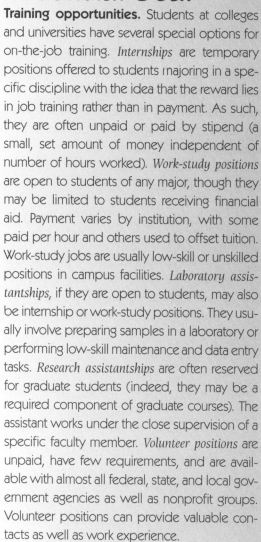

Essential Gear

Training opportunities. Students at colleges and universities have several special options for on-the-job training. *Internships* are temporary positions offered to students majoring in a specific discipline with the idea that the reward lies in job training rather than in payment. As such, they are often unpaid or paid by stipend (a small, set amount of money independent of number of hours worked). *Work-study positions* are open to students of any major, though they may be limited to students receiving financial aid. Payment varies by institution, with some paid per hour and others used to offset tuition. Work-study jobs are usually low-skill or unskilled positions in campus facilities. *Laboratory assistantships*, if they are open to students, may also be internship or work-study positions. They usually involve preparing samples in a laboratory or performing low-skill maintenance and data entry tasks. *Research assistantships* are often reserved for graduate students (indeed, they may be a required component of graduate courses). The assistant works under the close supervision of a specific faculty member. *Volunteer positions* are unpaid, have few requirements, and are available with almost all federal, state, and local government agencies as well as nonprofit groups. Volunteer positions can provide valuable contacts as well as work experience.

Find the path that's right for you. Switching to environmental science from most careers will involve some training, including a return to school. If you already have an associate's degree in the sciences, apply those credits to a bachelor's degree. If you are returning to school to earn a bachelor's degree, seek out a school that has an environmental science major. If you already have a bachelor's degree in the sciences, go back to school for a master's degree. If you are new to the sciences, enroll in basic science courses at your local community college while seeking out bachelor's degree programs that fit your goals. Being a student at any level will open up opportunities for necessary on-the-job experience, whether through assistantships, internships, or volunteer positions. Take advantage of these whenever you have the chance, and you will be ahead of the game when it comes to applying for jobs later.

Landmarks

If you are in your twenties . . . If you are an undergraduate, switch to an environmental science major. If this major is not available at your current institution, take as many science courses in as broad a range of disciplines as possible and consider transferring to a school with a respected environmental science program. If you are not currently in school, research degree programs in environmental science and apply. If you already have a degree in the sciences, begin seeking out entry level positions. If you have a bachelor's degree, apply to master's programs.

If you are in your thirties or forties . . . If you already work in the sciences or have a science degree, research current environmental science job openings. If you do not yet match their requirements for experience or education, return to school and look into applicable volunteer positions. If your degree is a bachelor's, apply to master's programs. If you are new to the sciences, seek out environmental science degree programs and return to school.

If you are in your fifties . . . If you have a science degree or career in the sciences, determine whether you are already qualified for an entry level environmental science position. If not, consider to what extent you will need to return to school or gain additional employment experience. If you have a bachelor's degree, apply to master's programs.

If you are over sixty . . . If you do not already have a science degree or a career in the sciences, you will need to return to school full-time for a degree in environmental science. Be certain that you are up to date on the latest technology, such as GPS, GIS, and computer modeling, as age-related discrimination is likely to manifest as questioning of your computer and other technological skills. You will need to maintain excellent physical condition and have very high stamina to be capable and competitive as well as to fight this same discrimination.

Further Resources

The **Society for Conservation Biology** is a professional membership organization for environmental scientists working in conservation. It hosts a Web site with many publications and resources, including a job board. http://www.conbio.org

The U.S. Department of the Interior's **Bureau of Land Management** has an extensive Web site that includes volunteer and employment opportunities. http://www.blm.gov

The **Student Conservation Association** has a Web site and mailing lists devoted to offering internships to students in the environmental sciences. http://www.thesca.org

AmeriCorps works to match volunteers from all walks of life to every imaginable kind of community service organization. Many positions offer scholarships as well as valuable experience working in chosen fields. The Web site includes a tool to search by area of interest and state. http://www.americorps.gov

Technical Writer

Technical Writer

Career Compasses

Get your bearings on what it takes to be a successful technical writer.

Communication Skills to give clear, concise, and useful instructions to a target audience (40%)

Organizational Skills to effectively research and write on a variety of topics (30%)

Caring about proper research techniques, accuracy, and educational communication (20%)

Ability to Manage Stress while marketing one's skills, researching projects, and meeting deadlines (10%)

Destination: Technical Writer

If you have ever assembled a toy or a piece of furniture, installed hardware or software, accessed a help page, or followed a Web tutorial, you have utilized the services of a technical writer. Technical writers use research and writing skills to explain technical subjects to target audiences. Usually this means writing such things as user manuals, tutorials, help pages, and other instructional materials.

Technical writers are not required to have expertise in any particular technological subject. Rather, they must have excellent research skills and written communication skills. They must have a certain talent for teaching, particularly for translating jargon and highly technical language into clear and understandable step-by-step instructions for end users. Empathy for their audience as well as the ability to communicate effectively with experts are critical. A technical writer will often consult with experts for information, clarification, and technical corrections, while also researching a topic in print and online. Excellent spelling and grammar are a must. It is extremely helpful to be a native speaker of the language in which you are writing, or to work closely with a native-speaking proofreader. Computer and Internet literacy are essential. Currently the majority of writing work is conducted over the Internet, from contracting projects to research to turning in manuscripts and, in many cases, the actual product is published online as well.

Essential Gear

Subject matter experts. You have been contracted to write the assembly instructions and user manual for the G3 Superfluous Monkey Widget Boondoggle 3000. Never heard of it? Never fear! The G3 Superfluous Monkey Widget Boondoggle 3000 engineer is here! It is not the technical writer's job to have extensive technical knowledge of any specific subject. It is the technical writer's job to have sharp research skills and the ability to reword information so that it is accurate yet understandable to the target audience. This often includes interviews with subject matter experts (SMEs). Staff technical writers may work closely with SMEs through all phases of design and development. Freelance technical writers may have to seek out SMEs through personal contacts or with their charm combined with online research skills. All technical writers, however, will eventually need to work with SMEs.

There is very little specific formal education required to become a technical writer. You must have writing and communication skills that range from excellent to perfect but how you go about proving these skills may vary. Many technical writers have a degree in English, journalism, or communications but many others do not. Having attended a college known for its strong emphasis on writing will help, as will all professional and published writing experience. A degree in liberal arts, a specific technical field, or design may situate you in a good position from which to begin a technical writing career. If you wish to specialize in writing for a particular technical field, such as software development or engineering, a degree in that field can be very helpful.

Journalism, fiction, and nonfiction publishing experience—including educational writing, copy writing, copyediting, and proofreading—may all help you to score that first technical writing gig. The most critical elements are to be able to write well for your specific audience, and to adjust your style based on your client's needs. Initially your audience will be companies seeking to hire a technical writer, as you gear your résumé and writing samples to them. You will need to strike a fine balance between showing that you are both capable and versatile, and to choose writing samples that are applicable to the job you are seeking. You must demonstrate that you have the skill set to perform technical writing, specifically. Once you have been hired, you will need to shift your focus to the specific audience, which will generally consist of end-users who need technical subjects explained to them on an elementary level. Your teaching and communication skills will be showcased far more than your ability to write engaging prose.

Some product developers and other companies hire staff technical writers. These writers produce user guides, product release notes, brochures, assembly instructions, tutorials, legal disclaimers, and the like. Some of these writers work in close communication with producers during the product development phase, and their work may include graphic design as well as communication with a large number of involved parties, from technicians and engineers to marketing specialists. Many technical writers work as independent contractors. These writers write on a work-for-hire, per-project basis, usually from home. Great self-discipline,

Essential Gear

Good documentation. So you are working from home, or you are working with SMEs but the information you have received is unintelligible or contradictory. How do you know what to do next? Have excellent research skills, which include knowing how to properly document your information. This means not only finding sources of information, but being able to sleuth out where your sources got their information. Particularly with online media, what at first appears to be a broad selection of sources often turns out, upon investigation, to be information from a single source repeated many times. If this single source is inaccurate, your own writing will be in trouble. Know how to cross reference sources. Standard practice for professional and academic writing is to check anything you put forth as fact with at least three independent sources.

time management, and organizational skills are necessary for this type of writing employment, as you will be simultaneously marketing yourself, running a home business, researching, writing, and keeping track of schedules and deadlines, sometimes for multiple projects.

Consistency of employment as well as annual income vary widely depending on the type of businesses you are employed by, the type of projects you work on, whether you work on a salaried or work-for-hire basis, and how often you are working. As of 2006, the median income for salaried writers fell between $48,000 and $58,000, while the reported range for all writers spanned from under $25,000 to over $90,000.

You Are Here

You can begin your journey to becoming a technical writer from many different locales.

Do you have writing experience? If you have verifiable writing experience, you are more than halfway to your new career. You will need to assemble a writing résumé and writing samples. A standard writing sample is usually in the area of 1,000 words or three pages, and standard practice is to submit two to three with a résumé. Keep your audience in mind when selecting writing samples, while selecting ones that show your skill and versatility. Be certain that your writing samples are perfect. Proofread them, then proofread them again. Have a friend proofread them as well. Nothing will work against you more than typos, grammatical errors, or a lack of clarity in your writing samples. Next you will need to approach your target audience. Online classified ads may be helpful, as may listings with professional organizations. Having a Web site that showcases some of your work may help, and personal contacts and word-of-mouth are often the most effective vehicles for employment.

Do you work in the sciences? If you have experience in the sciences you may be specially situated to write on specific topics. Even more importantly, you may have personal contacts who can help you get your foot in the door. If you already know people who hire technical writers, approach them with your résumé and writing samples. If you already know technical writers, seek their advice on breaking into the business, and make yourself available to them in the event that they have overflow work. If you do not yet have writing samples, or are not completely confident in your writing ability, enroll in classes in English writing and composition. Communications and graphic design classes may also give you a leading edge. If you are new to writing, do not skimp on furthering your education. Community colleges are excellent resources to hone your skills in the most affordable way possible. A large number of institutions now offer online and distance learning technical writing courses. Researching these with your particular needs in mind may also ease your way along your new career path.

Do you have a related degree? If you already have a degree in journalism, communications, English, design, advertising and marketing, or a technical field, you may be a step ahead. Liberal arts is also a valuable degree, in that you probably already have a selection of writing samples from which to choose, as well as excellent research and communication skills. Consider the writing you have already done and contacts you may have in the writing or technical fields, and use both as you compose your résumé and samples and begin seeking work.

Navigating the Terrain

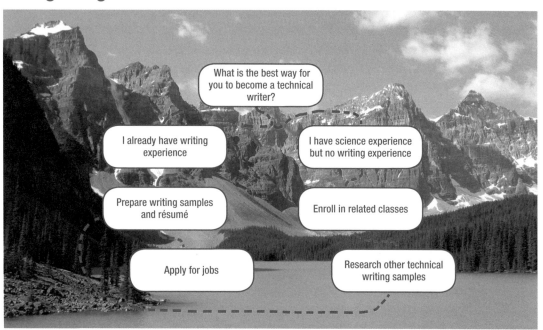

Notes from the Field

Suzanne Ahmed Leonora
Technical writer
Los Angeles, California

What were you doing before you decided to become a technical writer?

I was a cytogenetic technologist, a lab worker preparing and analyzing human chromosomes.

Why did you change your career?

Once I got a taste and an opportunity, I found that technical writing was a perfect fit for me: the learning, the analysis, the organization of information, the teaching aspects, the hours alone at my computer picking the right words and flow so that the reader would get everything.

How did you make the transition?

I got laid off, always a wonderful time for rethinking one's life. I was looking for work and saw an ad for part time technical writing at a company that made software for cytogenetic technology. I knew the users, the context, and the subject matter, and I had enjoyed writing the lab manual at my former job and standard operating procedures at a previous corporate lab job, so I applied, they hired me, and suddenly I was a tech writer.

What are the keys to success in your new career?

1) Fearlessness: an appetite for jumping into new situations, learning new subjects, and interviewing new subject matter experts.
2) Intelligence: an ability to understand all kinds of people and all kinds of subjects.
3) My highly analytical brain, which organizes information for both learning and explaining, readily returns to beginner's mind, and assesses the difference between what clients ask for and what they are ready for.
4) Flexibility to adapt to new markets and new assignments.
5) A very strong command of English acquired through both my highly analytical brain and an early acquaintance with well-written books. What with the deterioration of our schools, a word-geek like me

who doesn't need spell-check and knows the difference between "whether" and "if" is increasingly rare.

6) Confidence in my skills.

7) Good manners.

8) Outlines.

9) Communication with managers.

Since 9/11 and its economic aftermath, the number of positions for technical writers and the pay for those jobs has plummeted, while the technical knowledge allegedly required for those jobs has skyrocketed. Apparently decisions have been made to have engineers write documents, and to offer less documentation. My experience is that engineers do not want to write and, routinely, cannot write; that good documentation is a discrete skill not dependent on subject-matter knowledge, which can be acquired in every instance; and that documentation usually is inadequate rather than superfluous. Regardless, it is the plans of the hiring managers that determine the market, and, unsurprisingly, none of them are asking me what I think!

You always have to hit deadlines. Some of them are more comfortable than others but none are in your power. The assignment isn't always clear. Same for its justification. You have to write anyway. You can't always get what you need, information-wise. You have to write anyway.

You must focus keenly on the reader's experience, from their motivation for opening the document right through to what they do with the information, if anything. There is an inherent contradiction in technical writing: The information it contains is important, but the potential reader does not want to read it. One way to address this problem is to write even engineering documents as simply as possible; another is pop-up help in programs; screenshots are helpful for software. We are in transition from language-only documents to some future conveyance of information. The solution probably lies in visual presentations, i.e, cartoons and videos. We who function well in language-only will probably not be part of the solution; the end of our industry will probably be the beginning of a new one for graphic artists.

Organizing Your Expedition

Before you set out, know where you are going.

Decide on a destination. You have several options to pursue for employment: salaried or hourly employment as a staff technical writer, self-employment doing work-for-hire, or a combination of both. Decide which best fits your temperament and career goals. If you need to go into an office and have a set schedule in order to work efficiently, a staff position may be right for you. If you are very organized and motivated, enjoy working from home, have good marketing skills, and rarely fall victim to procrastination, taking on projects for various companies from your home office may be more your speed.

Scout the terrain. Where are you already strong? Where do you need to brush up on your skills? To be a professional writer you must be excellent at writing and proofreading. To be a technical writer, you must be very talented at translating technical language and information into a simple, educational form for end-users. Your computer skills must be strong. Word processing programs should be as natural to you as picking up a pencil, and you should be able and willing to navigate and learn new programs quickly and efficiently. You do not have to already be an expert in any technical or scientific area but you do have to be an expert in researching, collecting, and organizing data from print media, the Internet, and personal interviews.

Find the path that's right for you. Compare the strengths you already have to the type of assignments and employment situations you prefer. If your writing, research, or computer skills are not strong, enroll in classes at a community college or in online technical writing courses. Experience in related disciplines such as graphic design may make you more marketable. If you are a student of the sciences, take coursework in as broad a selection of subjects as possible, and seek out classes that involve a lot of writing. When you feel that you have a résumé and collection of writing samples that adequately demonstrate your abilities, begin seeking assignments. Keep an open mind when looking for work. Utilize personal contacts, online classifieds, and direct marketing to companies that hire technical writers. Most importantly, keep all doors open and use all available opportunities to continue developing your skills.

Landmarks

If you are in your twenties . . . If you are currently an undergraduate at a liberal arts college, begin selecting writing samples from your coursework with your résumé in mind. If you are an undergraduate at a more typical college or university, take courses in English writing and composition, communications, journalism, technical writing, and graphic design where available.

If you are in your thirties or forties . . . If you have writing experience or a liberal arts background, begin selecting writing samples. If you have science or technical experience select samples from the field you have been working in or, if you need to work on your writing skills, enroll in classes. Develop a strategy for marketing your talents. Use personal and professional contacts that you already have, while remembering that many of your contacts and employment opportunities will be developed online.

If you are in your fifties . . . The broader your educational experience, the more marketable you will be. Begin selecting your writing samples and developing your marketing strategy. Try to cull samples on a variety of topics. The more diversified your knowledge, the more work opportunities will be offered to you.

If you are over sixty . . . The advice given above applies to you as well. You are extremely unlikely to encounter age-related discrimination in this field but be certain that you are as computer and Internet literate as possible.

Further Resources

The **Society for Technical Communication** is a professional organization for technical writers and people in related writing careers and includes professional networking tools and educational information. http://www.stc.org

The **Chicago Manual of Style** sets the standard for professional writing, and is the ultimate reference guide for professional writers. Almost every writing assignment requires adherence to this manual.
http://www.chicagomanualofstyle.org

Writers Resources is a Web site that contains articles on many subjects meant to inspire and assist aspiring writers.
http://www.writersresources.com

Food Technologist

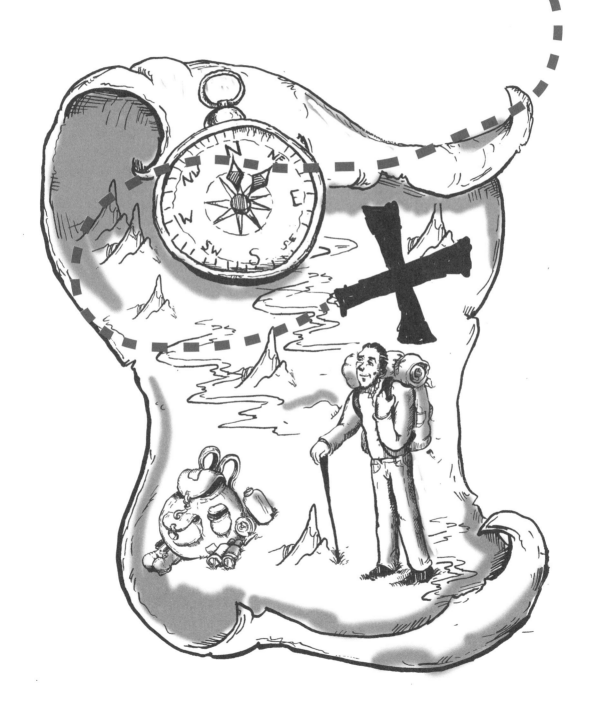

Food Technologist

Career Compasses

Get your bearings on what it takes to be a successful food technologist.

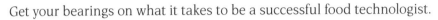

Relevant Knowledge of chemistry, biology, microbiology, biotechnology, physics, and food safety, applied to producing safe food (50%)

Organizational Skills to apply knowledge of the sciences and safety protocols (20%)

Caring about health, safety, and providing wholesome food (20%)

Communication Skills to work with other technicians as well as manufacturers (10%)

Destination: Food Technologist

Food technologists apply knowledge and techniques from a broad selection of scientific disciplines to the preservation, production, packaging, and transportation of food. They may work directly within agricultural operations, in processing and packaging plants, for investigative and enforcement agencies, as consultants, or in research and development.

Within agriculture, food technologists may work in the field of biotechnology, developing new strains of crop plants or food animals to produce higher yields, or they may develop techniques to improve the yields or desirable qualities of existing strains. Food technologists at the agricultural level may concern themselves with air, water, and soil pollution or with other contaminants in food, such as drug residues or dangerous microorganisms, in order to prevent passing these impurities into the human or animal food chain. In these roles, a background in animal science and husbandry, agricultural science, or horticulture is valuable.

Food technologists also work in food processing and product development. They may be called upon to develop new methods of processing or packaging, or to improve existing methods. Food technologists are also employed to inspect safety and sanitation procedures and protocols at processing and packaging plants, taking and analyzing samples to isolate chemical, material, or biological contaminants. Still others analyze samples of food products to determine their nutritional content.

Essential Gear

Blanching versus Pasteurization. Food processing procedures vary based on whether food is being prepared or preserved in small batches in a home or restaurant, or en masse by a processing plant for large-scale transport, distribution, and consumption. Both small-scale and mass production enterprises use methods of sanitizing and preserving food that are very similar in theory, but the specific methods vary based on the scale of production and distribution. In part, these distinctions are what separate culinary arts (small scale) from food technology (large scale). *Blanching* is a process whereby microorganisms are killed and enzymes are inactivated within a food product in preparation for storage, usually freezing. *Pasteurization* is a process meant to reduce the numbers of microbes in a food product in preparation for processing, transportation, and storage—usually by refrigeration or hermetic packaging.

Like chefs and cooks, food technologists work with cooking and preserving techniques such as canning and curing. Unlike chefs and cooks, however, their objective is not simply to create tasty foods but to prevent contamination, contagion, and spoilage by improving food preparation methods and sanitation. They also aim to improve upon existing methods of food handling, processing, and preservation in order to produce foodstuffs of higher nutritional quality and more stable storage life while decreasing the use of potentially harmful additives.

A bachelor's degree in agricultural science is a common way to enter the field of food technology, though a major in microbiology, biotechnology, biology, or chemistry is also excellent preparation. Some food technologists begin in such seemingly remote fields as physics or engineering, while others enter the field from culinary arts programs. Those who wish to eventually run research programs or teach at the university level are advised to seek a master's degree or doctorate. Food technologists must have working knowledge of cooking methods, food handling and preparation, and preservation techniques, from baking and blanching to distillation and pasteurization. At the same time, they must be skilled in statistics, data analysis, computer science, written communication, and interpersonal relations. Familiarity with business and marketing techniques will be helpful to those hoping to work with food processing and packaging companies, while a background in health and safety will be useful to those intending to fill investigative roles with government agencies. Animal science, horticulture and botany, and ethics are important for those intending to work in agricultural and biotechnology facilities. A background in culinary arts is suitable for some positions provided that coursework in the requisite sciences has been completed as well.

Essential Gear

USDA Requirements. The United States Department of Agriculture sets the standards for sanitation, safety, preparation, transportation, and storage of human food and animal feeds. These standards are extremely specific and include protocols for handling and storage of dry goods, fruits, vegetables, nuts, meat and fish, and milk and dairy products, as well as for export, domestic products, and organic certification. Any business that works with food or feeds can expect regular, unannounced visits from USDA inspectors, and everyone who works in the food or feed industry in any capacity should become familiar with USDA standards and follow them to the letter. In fact, as a budding food technologist, your dream job may be employment with the USDA.

Hours and work conditions will vary depending on the employer and type of work, from regular hours in a laboratory to irregular hours with frequent travel to processing plants, farms, and feedlots. Most positions will require working closely with other people, whether they be coworkers within a packaging facility or employees at a plant being inspected for compliance with sanitation codes. Good communication skills are essential in every case to keep one's job running smoothly.

Food technology is considered a stable employment area, neither experiencing enormous growth nor frightening decline, though current environmental impacts on farming are expected to slightly increase the demand for food technologists working within agriculture. As of 2006, average entry level earnings were reported at around $35,000 per year. Annual income in the field for established workers varied widely, ranging from about $36,000 to $80,000.

You Are Here

You can begin your journey to becoming a food technologist from a variety of locales.

Do you work in a related field? Any experience you have working in the sciences, in occupational or consumer health and safety, or in research and development, may help you transfer into a career as a food technologist. A number of universities, colleges, and vocational schools offer degrees or vocational certificates in food science. Most degrees in this discipline are offered at the associate's or the master's level. Bachelor's degrees are more often offered in nutrition, though bachelor's degree programs in food science are available at some schools. You must have a multidisciplinary background in the sciences as well as in agricultural and food processing methods in order to become a food technologist. If you already work in the culinary arts, you may have a broad understanding of food preparation issues, but need further education in the sciences as well as in supporting disciplines such as data analysis, statistics, and computer science.

Do you have a related degree? If you already have a degree in biology, microbiology, biotechnology, chemistry, animal science, agricultural science, horticulture, or the culinary arts you need to compare the educational experience you have in terms of actual college credits with the requirements for current job openings. For some positions, a related degree combined with work experience is sufficient. Others will train applicants on the job, while still others are very strict about having a degree specifically in agricultural science, food science, or nutrition. The requirements may vary greatly depending on which industries are active in your area, whether your state has licensing requirements, and the type of position you are seeking.

Navigating the Terrain

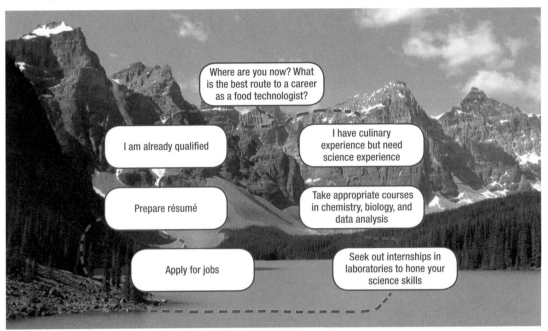

Organizing Your Expedition

Before you set out, know where you are going.

Decide on a destination. Consider your ultimate career goals. Do you wish to eventually head research and development programs or to teach? You will need to enroll in a master's degree program. If you aspire to the hands-on work of sampling, analyzing, or investigating, and do not wish to eventually take on the responsibility of developing programs or teaching, an advanced degree may not be your most expedient option. If you already have a related degree or a great deal of on-the-job experience, your quickest and easiest path may be to enroll in a vocational certificate program in food science. An associate's degree in food science, nutrition, or agricultural science may qualify you for an entry-level position as a technician. It may also provide excellent supplementary education and qualifications if you already have a bachelor's degree in a related discipline, but are new to food technology. Alternatively, if you have a related bachelor's degree, a food science master's degree may involve a similar time commitment to an associate's degree, but provide more options for future financial and status advancement in your new career.

Scout the terrain. Consider the options available in your area. Food science is not a common discipline and may not be available at your most convenient college or university. If you are interested in working with applied food technology or biotechnology within agriculture, most states have a land-grant college, that is, an institution that has been given control of public land in order to use it to create programs in agriculture, engineering, and the applied sciences. If good educational options are not available in your area, consider whether you are able and willing to move in order to pursue this path. Consider this also as you investigate employment options. What businesses and industries are active in your area? Is your region dominated by farms or feedlots, canning and processing plants, or small food-related businesses? Are public health agency offices in your area seeking food technologists to assist in inspections? Are there entrepreneurs seeking to apply nutritional and food science to the development and marketing of new healthful and organic products? Cast a wide net as you first investigate your future education and employment options, then draw it closed according to your interests and goals.

Find the path that's right for you. If you love the culinary arts but have limited experience with the sciences, consider your interests and academic needs carefully. Chances are that you will need to return to school. If you have a great deal of experience in the applied sciences, you may already be qualified for an entry-level position as a technician, from which you should be able to work your way up. If you currently work far from food and science, begin taking science courses and develop your personal curriculum as you determine the forum in which you most wish to apply your new skills.

Landmarks

If you are in your twenties . . . If you are currently an undergraduate, enroll in food or agricultural science courses. If these disciplines are not available at your current institution, take as many science courses as

Stories from the Field

Nicolas Appert
Food preservation engineer
Chalons-en-Champagne, France

Anyone familiar with food processing, preservation, and packaging, from home cooks to doctors of food science, is well-acquainted with the revolutionary practice of appertisation. Not so sure? The common term for appertisation is "canning."

Although food preservation methods such as salting, drying, smoking, and fermentation were used for centuries before confectioner Nicolas Appert achieved his breakthrough, none of these methods were capable of preserving all types of food in ready-to-eat forms. Inspired by a cash reward from Napoléon Bonaparte, Appert became a virtual firestorm of food processing research and development. After extensive experimentation, he discovered that boiling specially prepared, closed containers sealed them in such a way that spoilage of food was prevented as long as the seal remained intact. His choice to apply heat to the containers occurred well after the invention of the first microscope and the discovery of microorganisms, but prior to widespread acceptance of the germ theory of disease, and well before it was scientifically proven that many microorganisms can be killed with heat.

Appert's discovery, achieved in 1800, was funded for the purpose of providing rations to soldiers, as prior to this discovery many troops had minimal dried rations which they supplemented by forceful acquisition of food from residents in the areas they moved through or occupied—a poor public-relations choice and also insufficient for keeping a deployed army fed and healthy. Though the initial application was meant to serve a specific population, the method gained wide popularity and continues to be one of the primary forms of commercial and home food preservation today. His greatest coup was allegedly the canning of a whole sheep to great acclaim.

possible and consider transferring to a school that offers a food science major. If you are currently in culinary school, enroll in a science program concurrently or after you complete your course of study.

If you are in your thirties or forties . . . If you are not currently a student, investigate food and agricultural science degree programs and return to school. If you already have experience as a technician or technologist, determine the amount of supplemental education you will need to meet current employment requirements.

If you are in your fifties . . . The advice given above to people in their thirties or forties applies to you as well. If you have a bachelor's degree in a related field and wish to advance up the employment ladder, consider a master's degree program in your new discipline.

If you are over sixty . . . Consider whether you have the financial resources and stamina to return to school for a food or agricultural science degree. If you wish to get right to work, an associate's degree or vocational certificate combined with the experience you already have may be the option for you.

Further Resources

The **U. S. Department of Agriculture** offers information on a wide variety of topics, from legal regulations and standards in food processing to educational opportunities, biotechnology, biofuels, community development, environmental issues, and employment opportunities. http://www.usda.gov

The **Food and Drug Administration** of the Department of Health and Human Services employs technicians and investigators to inspect safety protocols, test products, and ensure compliance with federal health and safety regulations within the food processing industries. http://www.fda.gov

The **American Society of Agronomy** provides professional certification in agronomy, crop science, and soil science. http://www.agronomy.org

The **Institute of Food Technologists** is a professional membership organization that offers information on educational and employment opportunities for food technologists. http://www.ift.org/cms

Appendix A

# Going Solo: Starting Your Own Business

Starting your own business can be very rewarding—not only in terms of potential financial success, but also in the pleasure derived from building something from the ground up, contributing to the community, being your own boss, and feeling reasonably in control of your fate. However, business ownership carries its own obligations—both in terms of long hours of hard work and new financial and legal responsibilities. If you succeed in growing your business, your responsibilities only increase. Many new business owners come in expecting freedom only to find themselves chained tighter to their desks than ever before. Still, many business owners find greater satisfaction in their career paths than do workers employed by others.

The Internet has also changed the playing field for small business owners, making it easier than ever before to strike out on your own. While small mom-and-pop businesses such as hairdressers and grocery stores have always been part of the economic landscape, the Internet has made reaching and marketing to a niche easier and more profitable. This has made possible a boom in *microbusinesses*. Generally, a microbusiness is considered to have under ten employees. A microbusiness is also sometimes called a *SOHO* for "small office/home office."

The following appendix is intended to explain, in general terms, the steps in launching a small business, no matter whether it is selling your Web-design services or opening a pizzeria with business partners. It will also point out some of the things you will need to bear in mind. Remember also that the particular obligations of your municipality, state, province, or country may vary, and that this is by no means a substitute for doing your own legwork. Further suggested reading is listed at the end.

Crafting a Business Plan

It has often been said that success is 1 percent inspiration and 99 percent perspiration. However, the interface between the two can often be hard to achieve. The first step to taking your idea and making it reality is constructing a viable *business plan*. The purpose of a business plan is to think things all the way through, to make sure your ideas really are profitable, and to figure out the "who, what, when, where, why, and how" of your business. It fills in the details for three areas: your goals, why you think they are attainable, and how you plan to get to there. "You need to know where you're going before you take that first step," says Drew Curtis, successful Internet entrepreneur and founder of the popular newsfilter Fark.com.

Take care in writing your business plan. Generally, these documents contain several parts: An *executive summary* stating the essence of the plan; a *market summary* explaining how a need exists for the product and service you will supply and giving an idea of potential profitability by comparing your business to similar organizations; a *company description* which includes your products and services, why you think your organization will succeed, and any special advantages you have, as well as a description of *organization* and *management*; and your *marketing and sales strategy*. This last item should include market highlights and demographic information and trends that relate to your proposal. Also include a *funding request* for the amount of start-up capital you will need. This is supported by a section on *financials*, or the sort of cash flow you can expect, based on market analysis, projection, and comparison with existing companies. Other needed information, such as personal financial history, résumés, legal documents, or pictures of your product, can be placed in *appendices*.

Use your business plan to get an idea of how much startup money is necessary and to discipline your thinking and challenge your preconceived notions before you develop your cash flow. The business plan will tell you how long it will take before you turn a profit, which in turn is linked to how long it will before you will be able to pay back investors or a bank loan—which is something that anyone supplying you with money will want to know. Even if you are planning to subsist on grants or you are not planning on investment or even starting a for-profit company, the discipline imposed by the business plan is still the first step to organizing your venture.

A business plan also gives you a realistic view of your personal financial obligations. How long can you afford to live without regular income? How are you going to afford medical insurance? When will your business begin turning a profit? How much of a profit? Will you need to reinvest your profits in the business, or can you begin living off of them? Proper planning is key to success in any venture.

A final note on business plans: Take into account realistic expected profit minus realistic costs. Many small business owners begin by underestimating start-ups and variable costs (such as electricity bills), and then underpricing their product. This effectively paints them into a corner from which it is hard to make a profit. Allow for realistic market conditions on both the supply and the demand side.

Partnering Up

You should think long and hard about the decision to go into business with a partner (or partners). Whereas other people can bring needed capital, expertise, and labor to a business, they can also be liabilities. The questions you need to ask yourself are:

☞ Will this person be a full and equal partner? In other words, are they able to carry their own weight? Make a full and fair assessment of your potential partner's personality. Going into business with someone who lacks a work ethic, or prefers giving directions to working in the trenches, can be a frustrating experience.

☞ What will they contribute to the business? For instance, a partner may bring in start-up money, facilities, or equipment. However, consider if this is enough of a reason to bring them on board. You may be able to get the same advantages in another way—for instance, renting a garage rather than working out of your partner's. Likewise, doubling skill sets does not always double productivity.

☞ Do they have any liabilities? For instance, if your prospective partner has declared bankruptcy in the past, this can hurt your collective venture's ability to get credit.

☞ Will the profits be able to sustain all the partners? Many start-up ventures do not turn profits immediately, and what little they do produce can be spread thin amongst many partners. Carefully work out the math.

Also bear in mind that going into business together can put a strain on even the best personal relationships. No matter whether it is family, friends, or strangers, keep everything very professional with written agreements regarding these investments. Get everything in writing, and be clear where obligations begin and end. "It's important to go into business with the right people," says Curtis. "If you don't—if it degrades into infighting and petty bickering—it can really go south quickly."

Incorporating. . . or Not

Think long and hard about incorporating. Starting a business often requires a fairly large—and risky—financial investment, which in turn exposes you to personal liability. Furthermore, as your business grows, so does your risk. Incorporating can help you shield yourself from this liability. However, it also has disadvantages.

To begin with, incorporating is not necessary for conducting professional transactions such as obtaining bank accounts and credit. You can do this as a sole proprietor, partnership, or simply by filing a DBA ("doing business as") statement with your local court (also known as "trading as" or an "assumed business name"). The DBA is an accounting entity that facilitates commerce and keeps your business' money separate from your own. However, the DBA does not shield you from responsibility if your business fails. It is entirely possible to ruin your credit, lose your house, and have your other assets seized in the unfortunate event of bankruptcy.

The purpose of incorporating is to shield yourself from personal financial liability. In case the worst happens, only the business' assets can be taken. However, this is not always the best solution. Check your local laws: Many states have laws that prevent a creditor from seizing a non-incorporated small business' assets in case of owner bankruptcy. If you are a corporation, however, the things you use to do business that are owned by the corporation—your office equipment, computers, restaurant refrigerators, and other essential equipment—may be seized by creditors, leaving you no way to work yourself out of debt. This is why it is imperative to consult with a lawyer.

There are other areas in which being a corporation can be an advantage, such as business insurance. Depending on your business needs, insurance can be for a variety of things: malpractice, against delivery failures or spoilage, or liability against defective products or accidents. Furthermore, it is easier to hire employees, obtain credit, and buy health insurance as an organization than as an individual. However, on the downside, corporations are subject to specific and strict laws concerning management and ownership. Again, you should consult with a knowledgeable legal expert.

Among the things you should discuss with your legal expert are the advantages and disadvantages of incorporating in your jurisdiction and which type of incorporation is best for you. The laws on liability and how much of your profit will be taken away in taxes vary widely by state and country. Generally, most small businesses owners opt for *limited liability companies* (LLCs), which gives them more control and a more flexible management structure. (Another possibility is a *limited liability partnership*, or *LLP*, which is especially useful for professionals such as doctors and lawyers.) Finally, there is the *corporation*, which is characterized by transferable ownerships shares, perpetual succession, and, of course, limited liability.

Most small businesses are sole proprietorships, partnerships, or privately-owned corporations. In the past, not many incorporated, since it was necessary to have multiple owners to start a corporation. However, this is changing, since it is now possible in many states for an individual to form a corporation. Note also that the form your business takes is usually not set in stone: A sole proprietorship or partnership can switch to become an LLC as it grows and the risks increase; furthermore, a successful LLC can raise capital by changing its structure to become a corporation and selling stock.

Legal Issues

Many other legal issues besides incorporating (or not) need to be addressed before you start your business. It is impossible to speak directly to every possible business need in this brief appendix, since regulations, licenses, and health and safety codes vary by industry and locality. A restaurant in Manhattan, for instance, has to deal not only with the usual issues such as health inspectors, and the state liquor board, but obscure regulations such as New York City's cabaret laws, which prohibit dancing without a license in a place where alcohol is sold. An asbestos-abatement company, on the other hand, has a very different set of standards it has to abide by, including federal regulations. Researching applicable laws is part of starting up any business.

Part of being a wise business owner is knowing when you need help. There is software available for things like bookkeeping, business plans, and Web site creation, but generally, consulting with a knowledgeable professional—an accountant or a lawyer (or both)—is the smartest move. One of the most common mistakes is believing that just because you have expertise in the technical aspects of a certain field, you know all about running a business in that field. Whereas some people may balk at the expense, by suggesting the best way to deal with possible problems, as well as cutting through red tape and seeing possible pitfalls that you may not even have been aware of, such professionals usually more than make up for their cost. After all, they have far more experience at this than does a first-time business owner!

Financial

Another necessary first step in starting a business is obtaining a bank account. However, having the account is not as important as what you do with it. One of the most common problems with small businesses is undercapitalization—especially in brick-and-mortar businesses that sell or make something, rather than service-based businesses. The rule of thumb is that you should have access to money equal to your first year's anticipated profits, plus start-up expenses. (Note that this is not the same as having the money on hand—see the discussion on lines of credit, below.) For instance, if your annual rent, salaries, and equipment will cost $50,000 and you expect $25,000 worth of profit in your first year, you should have access to $75,000 worth of financing.

You need to decide what sort of financing you will need. Small business loans have both advantages and disadvantages. They can provide critical start-up credit, but in order to obtain one, your personal credit will need to be good, and you will, of course, have to pay them off with interest. In general, the more you and your partners put into the business yourselves, the more credit lenders will be willing to extend to you.

Equity can come from your own personal investment, either in cash or an equity loan on your home. You may also want to consider bringing on partners—at least limited financial partners—as a way to cover start-up costs.

It is also worth considering obtaining a line of credit instead of a loan. A loan is taken out all at once, but with a line of credit, you draw on the money as you need it. This both saves you interest payments and means that you have the money you need when you need it. Taking out too large of a loan can be worse than having no money at all! It just sits there collecting interest—or, worse, is spent on something utterly unnecessary—and then is not around when you need it most.

The first five years are the hardest for any business venture; your venture has about double the usual chance of closing in this time (1 out of 6, rather than 1 out of 12). You will probably have to tighten your belt at home, as well as work long hours and keep careful track of your business expenses. Be careful with your money. Do not take unnecessary risks, play it conservatively, and always keep some capital in reserve for emergencies. The hardest part of a new business, of course, is the learning curve of figuring out what, exactly, you need to do to make a profit, and so the best advice is to have plenty of savings—or a job to provide income—while you learn the ropes.

One thing you should not do is count on venture capitalists or "angel investors," that is, businesspeople who make a living investing on other businesses in the hopes that their equity in the company will increase in value. Venture capitalists have gotten something of a reputation as indiscriminate spendthrifts due to some poor choices made during the dot-com boom of the late 1990s, but the fact is that most do not take risks on unproven products. Rather, they are attracted to young companies that have the potential to become regional or national powerhouses and give better-than-average returns. Nor are venture capitalists endless sources of money; rather, they are savvy businesspeople who are usually attracted to companies that have already experienced a measure of success. Therefore, it is better to rely on your own resources until you have proven your business will work.

Bookkeeping 101

The principles of double-entry bookkeeping have not changed much since its invention in the fifteenth century: one column records debits, and one records credits. The trick is *doing* it. As a small business owner, you need to be disciplined and meticulous at recording your finances. Thankfully, today there is software available that can do everything from tracking payables and receivables to running checks and generating reports.

Honestly ask yourself if you are the sort of person who does a good job keeping track of finances. If you are not, outsource to a bookkeeping company or hire someone to come in once or twice a week to enter invoices and generate checks for you. Also remember that if you have employees or even freelancers, you will have to file tax forms for them at the end of the year.

Another good idea is to have an accountant for your business to handle advice and taxes (federal, state, local, sales tax, etc.). In fact, consulting with a certified public accountant is a good idea in general, since they are usually aware of laws and rules that you have never even heard of.

Finally, keep your personal and business accounting separate. If your business ever gets audited, the first thing the IRS looks for is personal expenses disguised as business expenses. A good accountant can help you to know what are legitimate business expenses. Everything you take from the business account, such as payroll and reimbursement, must be recorded and classified.

Being an Employer

Know your situation regarding employees. To begin with, if you have any employees, you will need an Employer Identification Number (EIN), also sometimes called a Federal Tax Identification Number. Getting an EIN is simple: You can fill out IRS form SS-4, or complete the process online at http://www.irs.gov.

Having employees carries other responsibilities and legalities with it. To begin with, you will need to pay payroll taxes (otherwise known as "withholding") to cover income tax, unemployment insurance, Social Security, and Medicare, as well as file W-2 and W-4 forms with the government. You will also be required to pay worker's compensation insurance, and will probably also want to find medical insurance. You are also required to abide by your state's nondiscrimination laws. Most states require you to post nondiscrimination and compensation notices in a public area.

Many employers are tempted to unofficially hire workers "off the books." This can have advantages, but can also mean entering a legal gray area. (Note, however, this is different from hiring freelancers, a temp employed by another company, or having a self-employed professional such as an accountant or bookkeeper come in occasionally to provide a service.) It is one thing to hire the neighbor's teenage son on a one-time basis to help you move some boxes, but quite another to have full-time workers working on a cash-and-carry basis. Regular wages must be noted in the accounts, and gaps may be questioned in the event of an audit. If the workers are injured on the job, you are not covered by worker's comp, and are thus vulnerable to lawsuits. If the workers you hired are not legal residents, you can also be liable for civil and criminal penalties. In general, it is best to keep your employees as above-board as possible.

Building a Business

Good business practices are essential to success. First off, do not overextend yourself. Be honest about what you can do and in what time frame. Secondly, be a responsible business owner. In general, if there is a problem, it is best to explain matters honestly to your clients than to leave them without word and wondering. In the former case, there is at least the possibility of salvaging your reputation and credibility.

Most business is still built by personal contacts and word of mouth. It is for this reason that maintaining your list of contacts is an essential practice. Even if a particular contact may not be useful at a particular moment, a future opportunity may present itself—or you may be able to send someone else to them. Networking, in other words, is as important when you are the boss as when you are looking for a job yourself. As the owner of a company, having a network means getting services on better terms, knowing where to go if you need help with a particular problem, or simply being in the right place at the right time to exploit an opportunity. Join professional organizations, the local Chamber of Commerce, clubs and community organizations, and learn to play golf. And remember—never burn a bridge.

Advertising is another way to build a business. Planning an ad campaign is not as difficult as you might think: You probably already know your media market and business community. The trick is applying it. Again, go with your instincts. If you never look twice at your local weekly, other people probably do not, either. If you are in a high-tourist area, though, local tourist maps might be a good way to leverage your marketing dollar. Ask other people in your area or market who have businesses similar to your own. Depending on your focus, you might want to consider everything from AM radio or local TV networks, to national trade publications, to hiring a PR firm for an all-out blitz. By thinking about these questions, you can spend your advertising dollars most effectively.

Nor should you underestimate the power of using the Internet to build your business. It is a very powerful tool for small businesses, potentially reaching vast numbers of people for relatively little outlay of money. Launching a Web site has become the modern equivalent of hanging out your shingle. Even if you are primarily a brick-and-mortar business, a Web presence can still be an invaluable tool—your store or offices will show up on Google searches, plus customers can find directions to visit you in person. Furthermore, the Internet offers the small-business owner many useful tools. Print and design services, order fulfillment, credit card processing, and networking—both personal and in terms of linking to other sites—are all available online. Web advertising can be useful, too, either by advertising on specialty sites that appeal to your audience, or by using services such as Google AdWords.

Amateurish print ads, TV commercials, and Web sites do not speak well of your business. Good media should be well-designed, well-edited, and well-put together. It need not, however, be expensive. Shop around and, again, use your network.

Flexibility is also important. "In general, a business must adapt to changing conditions, find new customers and find new products or services that customers need when the demand for their older products or services diminishes," says James Peck, a Long Island, New York, entrepreneur. In other words, if your original plan is not working out, or if demand falls, see if you can parlay your experience, skills, and physical plant into meeting other needs. People are not the only ones who can change their path in life; organizations can, too.

A Final Word

In business, as in other areas of life, the advice of more experienced people is essential. "I think it really takes three businesses until you know what you're doing," Drew Curtis confides. "I sure didn't know what I was doing the first time." Listen to what others have to say, no matter whether it is about your Web site or your business plan. One possible solution is seeking out a mentor, someone who has previously launched a successful venture in this field. In any case, before taking any step, ask as many people as many questions as you can. Good advice is invaluable.

Further Resources

American Independent Business Alliance
http://www.amiba.net

American Small Business League
http://www.asbl.com

IRS Small Business and Self-Employed One-Stop Resource
http://www.irs.gov/businesses/small/index.html

The Riley Guide: Steps in Starting Your Own Business
http://www.rileyguide.com/steps.html

Small Business Administration
http://www.sba.gov

Appendix B

Outfitting Yourself for Career Success

As you contemplate a career shift, the first component is to assess your interests. You need to figure out what makes you tick, since there is a far greater chance that you will enjoy and succeed in a career that taps into your passions, inclinations, natural abilities, and training. If you have a general idea of what your interests are, you at least know in which direction you want to travel. You may know you want to simply switch from one sort of nursing to another, or change your life entirely and pursue a dream you have always held. In this case, you can use a specific volume of The Field Guides to Finding a New Career to discover which position to target. If you are unsure of the direction you want to take, well, then the entire scope of the series is open to you! Browse through to see what appeals to you, and see if it matches with your experience and abilities.

The next step you should take is to make a list—do it once in writing—of the skills you have used in a position of responsibility that transfer to the field you are entering. People in charge of interviewing and hiring may well understand that the skills they are looking for in a new hire are used in other fields, but you must spell it out. Most job descriptions are partly a list of skills. Map your experience into that, and very early in your contacts with a prospective employer explicitly address how you acquired your relevant skills. Pick a relatively unimportant aspect of the job to be your ready answer for where you would look forward to learning within the organization, if this seems essentially correct. When you transfer into a field, softly acknowledge a weakness while relating your readiness to learn, but never lose sight of the value you offer both in your abilities and in the freshness of your perspective.

Energy and Experience

The second component in career-switching success is energy. When Jim Fulmer was 61, he found himself forced to close his piano-repair business. However, he was able to parlay his knowledge of music, pianos, and the musical instruments industry into another job as a sales representative for a large piano manufacturer, and quickly built up a clientele of musical-instrument retailers throughout the East Coast. Fulmer's experience highlights another essential lesson for career-changers: There are plenty of opportunities out there, but jobs will not come to you—especially the career-oriented, well-paying ones. You have to seek them out.

Jim Fulmer's case also illustrates another important point: Former training and experience can be a key to success. "Anyone who has to make a career change in any stage of life has to look at what skills they have acquired but may not be aware of," he says. After all, people can more easily change into careers similar to the ones they are leaving. Training and experience also let you enter with a greater level of seniority, provided you have the other necessary qualifications. For instance, a nurse who is already experienced with administering drugs and their benefits and drawbacks, and who is also graced with the personality and charisma to work with the public, can become a pharmaceutical company sales representative.

Unlock Your Network

The next step toward unlocking the perfect job is networking. The term may be overused, but the idea is as old as civilization. More than other animals, humans need one another. With the Internet and telephone, never in history has it been easier to form (or revive) these essential links. One does not have to gird oneself and attend reunion-type events (though for many this is a fine tactic)—but keep open to opportunities to meet people who may be friendly to you in your field. Ben Franklin understood the principle well—*Poor Richard's Almanac* is something of a treatise on the importance of cultivating what Franklin called "friendships" with benefactors. So follow in the steps of the founding fathers and make friends to get ahead. Remember: helping others feels good; it's often the receiving that gets a little tricky. If you know someone particularly well-connected in your field, consider tapping one or two less important connections first so that you make the most of the important one. As you proceed, keep your strengths foremost in your mind because the glue of commerce is mutual interest.

Eighty percent of job openings are *never advertised*, and, according to the U.S. Bureau of Labor statistics, more than half of all employees landed their jobs through networking. Using your personal contacts is far more efficient and effective than trusting your résumé to the Web.

On the Web, an employer needs to sort through tens of thousands—or millions—of résumés. When you direct your application to one potential employer, you are directing your inquiry to one person who already knows you. The personal touch is everything: Human beings are social animals, programmed to "read" body language; we are naturally inclined to trust those we meet in person, or who our friends and coworkers have recommended. While Web sites can be useful (for looking through help-wanted ads, for instance), expecting employers to pick you out of the slush pile is as effective as throwing your résumé into a black hole.

Do not send your résumé out just to make yourself feel like you're doing something. The proper way to go about things is to employ discipline and order, and then to apply your charm. Begin your networking efforts by making a list of people you can talk to: colleagues, coworkers, and supervisors, people you have had working relationship with, people from church, athletic teams, political organizations, or other community groups, friends, and relatives. You can expand your networking opportunities by following the suggestions in each chapter of the volumes. Your goal here is not so much to land a job as to expand your possibilities and knowledge: Though the people on your list may not be in the position to help you themselves, they might know someone who is. Meeting with them might also help you understand traits that matter and skills that are valued in the field in which you are interested. Even if the person is a potential employer, it is best to phrase your request as if you were seeking information: "You might not be able to help me, but do you know someone I could talk to who could tell me more about what it is like to work in this field?" Being hungry gives one impression, being desperate quite another.

Keep in mind that networking is a two-way street. If you meet someone who has an opening that is not right for you, but you could recommend someone else, you have just added to your list two people who will be favorably disposed toward you in the future. Also, bear in mind that *you* can help people in *your* old field, thus adding to your own contacts list.

Networking is especially important to the self-employed or those who start their own businesses. Many people in this situation begin because they either recognize a potential market in a field that they are familiar with, or because full-time employment in this industry is no longer a possibility. Already being well-established in a field can help, but so can asking connections for potential work and generally making it known that you are ready, willing, and able to work. Working your professional connections, in many cases, is the *only* way to establish yourself. A free-lancer's network, in many cases, is like a spider's web. The spider casts out many strands, since he or she never knows which one might land the next meal.

Dial-Up Help

In general, it is better to call contacts directly than to e-mail them. E-mails are easy for busy people to ignore or overlook, even if they do not mean to. Explain your situation as briefly as possible (see the discussion of the "elevator speech"), and ask if you could meet briefly, either at their office or at a neutral place such as a café. (Be sure that you pay the bill in such a situation—it is a way of showing you appreciate their time and effort.) If you get someone's voicemail, give your "elevator speech" and then say you will call back in a few days to follow up—and then do so. If you reach your contact directly and they are too busy to speak or meet with you, make a definite appointment to call back at a later date. Be persistent, but not annoying.

Once you have arranged a meeting, prep yourself. Look at industry publications both in print and online, as well as news reports (here, GoogleNews, which lets you search through online news reports, can be very handy). Having up-to-date information on industry trends shows that you are dedicated, knowledgeable, and focused. Having specific questions on employers and requests for suggestions will set you apart from the rest of the job-hunting pack. Knowing the score—for instance, asking about the value of one sort of certification instead of another—pegs you as an "insider," rather than a dilettante, someone whose name is worth remembering and passing along to a potential employer.

Finally, set the right mood. Here, a little self-hypnosis goes a long way: Look at yourself in the mirror, and tell yourself that you are an enthusiastic, committed professional. Mood affects confidence and performance. Discipline your mind so you keep your perspective and self-respect. Nobody wants to hire someone who comes across as insincere, tells a sob story, or is still in the doldrums of having lost their previous job. At the end of any networking meeting, ask for someone else who might be able to help you in your journey to finding a position in this field, either with information or a potential job opening.

Get a Lift

When you meet with a contact in person (as well as when you run into anyone by chance who may be able to help you), you need an "elevator speech" (so-named because it should be short enough to be delivered during an elevator ride from a ground level to a high floor). This is a summary in which, in less than two minutes, you give them a clear impression of who you are, where you come from, your experience and goals, and why you are on the path you are on. The motto above Plato's Academy holds true: Know Thyself (this is where our Career Compasses and guides will help you). A long and rambling "elevator story" will get you nowhere. Furthermore, be positive: Neither a sad-sack story nor a tirade explaining how everything that went wrong in your old job is someone else's fault will get you anywhere. However, an honest explanation of a less-than-fortunate circumstance, such as a decline in business forcing an office closure, needing to change residence to a place where you are not qualified to work in order to further your spouse's career, or needing to work fewer hours in order to care for an ailing family member, is only honest.

An elevator speech should show 1) you know the business involved; 2) you know the company; 3) you are qualified (here, try to relate your education and work experience to the new situation); and 4) you are goal-oriented, dependable, and hardworking. Striking a balance is important; you want to sound eager, but not overeager. You also want to show a steady work experience, but not that you have been so narrowly focused that you cannot adjust. Most important is emphasizing what you can do for the company. You will be surprised how much information you can include in two minutes. Practice this speech in front of a mirror until you have the key points down perfectly. It should sound natural, and you should come across as friendly, confident, and assertive. Finally, remember eye contact! Good eye contact needs to be part of your presentation, as well as your everyday approach when meeting potential employers and leads.

Get Your Résumé Ready

Everyone knows what a résumé is, but how many of us have really thought about how to put one together? Perhaps no single part of the job search is subject to more anxiety—or myths and misunderstandings—than this 8 ½-by-11-inch sheet of paper.

On the one hand, it is perfectly all right for someone—especially in certain careers, such as academia—to have a résumé that is more than one page. On the other hand, you do not need to tell a future employer *everything*. Trim things down to the most relevant; for a 40-year-old to mention an internship from two decades ago is superfluous. Likewise, do not include irrelevant jobs, lest you seem like a professional career-changer.

Tailor your descriptions of your former employment to the particular position you are seeking. This is not to say you should lie, but do make your experience more appealing. If the job you're looking for involves supervising other people, say if you have done this in the past; if it involves specific knowledge or capabilities, mention that you possess these qualities. In general, try to make your past experience seem similar to what you are seeking.

The standard advice is to put your Job Objective at the heading of the résumé. An alternative to this is a Professional Summary, which some recruiters and employers prefer. The difference is that a Job Objective mentions the position you are seeking, whereas a Professional Summary mentions your background (e.g. "Objective: To find a position as a sales representative in agribusiness machinery" versus "Experienced sales representative; strengths include background in agribusiness, as well as building team dynamics and market expansion"). Of course, it is easy to come up with two or three versions of the same document for different audiences.

The body of the résumé of an experienced worker varies a lot more than it does at the beginning of your career. You need not put your education or your job experience first; rather, your résumé should emphasize your strengths. If you have a master's degree in a related field, that might want to go before your unrelated job experience. Conversely, if too much education will harm you, you might want to bury that under the section on professional presentations you have given that show how good you are at communicating. If you are currently enrolled in a course or other professional development, be sure to note this (as well as your date of expected graduation). A résumé is a study of blurs, highlights, and jewels. You blur everything you must in order to fit the description of your experience to the job posting. You highlight what is relevant from each and any of your positions worth mentioning. The jewels are the little headers and such—craft them, since they are what is seen first.

You may also want to include professional organizations, work-related achievements, and special abilities, such as your fluency in a foreign language. Also mention your computer software qualifications and capabilities, especially if you are looking for work in a technological field or if you are an older job-seeker who might be perceived as behind the technology curve. Including your interests or family information might or might not be a good idea—no one really cares about your bridge club, and in fact they might worry that your marathon training might take away from your work commitments, but, on the other hand, mentioning your golf handicap or three children might be a good idea if your potential employer is an avid golfer or is a family woman herself.

You can either include your references or simply note, "References available upon request." However, be sure to ask your references' permission to use their names and alert them to the fact that they may be contacted before you include them on your résumé! Be sure to include name, organization, phone number, and e-mail address for each contact.

Today, word processors make it easy to format your résumé. However, beware of prepackaged résumé "wizards"—they do not make you stand out in the crowd. Feel free to strike out on your own, but remember the most important thing in formatting a résumé is consistency. Unless you have a background in typography, do not get too fancy. Finally, be sure to have someone (or several people!) read your résumé over for you.

For more information on résumé writing, check out Web sites such as http://www.résumé.monster.com.

Craft Your Cover Letter

It is appropriate to include a cover letter with your résumé. A cover letter lets you convey extra information about yourself that does not fit or is not always appropriate in your résumé, such as why you are no longer working in your original field of employment. You can and should also mention the name of anyone who referred you to the job. You can go into some detail about the reason you are a great match, given the job description. Also address any questions that might be raised in the potential employer's mind (for instance, a gap in employment). Do not, however, ramble on. Your cover letter should stay focused on your goal: To offer a strong, positive impression of yourself and persuade the hiring manager that you are worth an interview. Your cover letter gives you a chance to stand out from the other applicants and sell yourself. In fact, according to a CareerBuilder.

com survey, 23 percent of hiring managers say a candidate's ability to relate his or her experience to the job at hand is a top hiring consideration.

Even if you are not a great writer, you can still craft a positive yet concise cover letter in three paragraphs: An introduction containing the specifics of the job you are applying for; a summary of why you are a good fit for the position and what you can do for the company; and a closing with a request for an interview, contact information, and thanks. Remember to vary the structure and tone of your cover letter—do not begin every sentence with "I."

Ace Your Interview

In truth, your interview begins well before you arrive. Be sure to have read up well on the company and its industry. Use Web sites and magazines—http://www.hoovers.com offers free basic business information, and trade magazines deliver both information and a feel for the industries they cover. Also, do not neglect talking to people in your circle who might know about trends in the field. Leave enough time to digest the information so that you can give some independent thought to the company's history and prospects. You don't need to be an expert when you arrive to be interviewed; but you should be comfortable. The most important element of all is to be poised and relaxed during the interview itself. Preparation and practice can help a lot.

Be sure to develop well-thought-through answers to the following, typical interview openers and standard questions.

☞ Tell me about yourself. (Do not complain about how unsatisfied you were in your former career, but give a brief summary of your applicable background and interest in the particular job area.) If there is a basis to it, emphasize how much you love to work and how you are a team player.

☞ Why do you want this job? (Speak from the brain, and the heart—of course you want the money, but say a little here about what you find interesting about the field and the company's role in it.)

☞ What makes you a good hire? (Remember here to connect the company's needs and your skill set. Ultimately, your selling points probably come down to one thing: you will make your employer money. You want the prospective hirer to see that your skills are valuable not to the world in general but to this specific company's bottom line. What can you do for them?)

☞ What led you to leave your last job? (If you were fired, still try to say something positive, such as, "The business went through a challenging time, and some of the junior marketing people were let go.")

Practice answering these and other questions, and try to be genuinely positive about yourself, and patient with the process. Be secure but not cocky; don't be shy about forcing the focus now and then on positive contributions you have made in your working life—just be specific. As with the elevator speech, practice in front of the mirror.

A couple pleasantries are as natural a way as any to start the actual interview, but observe the interviewer closely for any cues to fall silent and formally begin. Answer directly; when in doubt, finish your phrase and look to the interviewer. Without taking command, you can always ask, "Is there more you would like to know?" Your attentiveness will convey respect. Let your personality show too—a positive attitude and a grounded sense of your abilities will go a long way to getting you considered. During the interview, keep your cell phone off and do not look at your watch. Toward the end of your meeting, you may be asked whether you have any questions. It is a good idea to have one or two in mind. A few examples follow:

☞ "What makes your company special in the field?"
☞ "What do you consider the hardest part of this position?"
☞ "Where are your greatest opportunities for growth?"
☞ "Do you know when you might need anything further from me?"

Leave discussion of terms for future conversations. Make a cordial, smooth exit.

Remember to Follow Up

Send a thank-you note. Employers surveyed by CareerBuilder.com in 2005 said it matters. About 15 percent said they would not hire someone who did not follow up with a thanks. And almost 33 percent would think less of a candidate. The form of the note does not much matter—if you know a manager's preference, use it. Otherwise, just be sure to follow up.

A

Accreditation Board for Engineering and Technology, 56

Accrediting Bureau of Health Education Schools, 12

age group landmarks
atmospheric scientist, 22–23
chemist/materials scientist, 64–66
environmental scientist, 88
food technologist, 107–109
geoscientist, 33–34
grant writer, 43–46
health/safety technician, 55–56
laboratory technician, 11
science teacher, 75–76
technical writer, 98

American Association of Petroleum Geologists, 35

American Chemical Society, 66

American Federation of Teachers, 77

American Geological Institute, 34

American Independent Business Alliance, 123

American Industrial Hygiene Association, 56

American Meteorological Society, 21–22, 23

American Small Business League, 123

American Society of Agronomy, 109

AmeriCorps, 89

Argonne National Laboratory, 66

atmospheric scientist, xii, 14–23
age group landmarks, 22–23
career compasses, 14
climatology and, 16
education/training, 16, 21–22
essential gear, 15, 16
field notes, 20
internships/volunteering and, 16
job description, 14–17
job prospects, 17
meteorologists and, 15
related work experience, 18, 21
resources, 21–22, 23
skills/qualifications, 15, 17–19
specialization and, 17–18, 19–20
transition expedition, 19–22

B

bookkeeping, 119–120

Bureau of Labor Statistics, vii, viii

Bureau of Land Management, 89

business, starting own, 113–123
bookkeeping for, 119–120
building, 121–122
employer in, being, 120–121
financial issues in, 118–119
incorporation of, 116–117
legal issues in, 117–118
partnership in, 115–116
plan, 113–115
resources for, 123
testimonial on, 127–128

C

career(s)
finding new, vii–viii
science, xi–xiv
successful, 127–136

career compasses
atmospheric scientist, 14
chemist/materials scientist, 58
environmental scientist, 79
food technologist, 102
geoscientist, 25
grant writer, 37
health/safety technician, 48
laboratory technician, 2
science teacher, 68
technical writer, 91

chemist/materials scientist, 58–66
    age group landmarks, 64–66
    career compasses, 58
    education/training, 60, 61–62, 63
    essential gear, 59, 60
    field notes, 64–65
    job description, 58–60
    job prospects, 59–60
    related work experience, 61, 62
    resources, 66
    salary/wages, 60
    skills/qualifications, 61
    specialization and, 59, 62
    transition expedition, 62–64
Chicago Manual of Style, 100
climatology, 16
Clinical Laboratory Management Association,
    12
Council on Certification of Health,
    Environmental, and Safety Technologists, 56
cover letter, 133–134
credit, financing and, 118–119

D
Department of Agriculture, U.S. (USDA), 109
Department of Energy, Argonne National
    Laboratory, U.S., 66
Department of Health and Human Services,
    U.S., 46

E
education/training, xiii–xiv
    atmospheric scientist, 16, 21–22
    chemist/materials scientist and, 60, 61–62,
        63
    environmental scientist, 80, 83, 87
    food technologist, 103–104, 105
    geoscientist, 26–27, 28, 33
    grant writer, 41, 43
    health/safety technician, 51, 52

    laboratory technician, 5, 6, 10
    science teacher, 70, 71
    technical writer, 92–93, 95
elevator speech, 131
employer, starting own business as, 120–121
energy, 127–128
environmental scientist, 79–89
    age group landmarks, 88
    career compasses, 79
    education/training, 80, 83, 87
    essential gear, 80, 87
    field notes, 84–86
    job description, 79–82
    resources, 89
    salary/wages, 82
    skills/qualifications, 81, 82–83
    specialization and, 80, 86
    transition expedition, 86–88
equity, business and, 118
essential gear
    atmospheric scientist, 15, 16
    chemist/materials scientist and, 59, 60
    environmental scientist, 80, 87
    food technologist, 103, 104
    geoscientist, 26, 32
    grant writer, 38, 39
    health/safety technician, 50, 51
    laboratory technician, 3, 4
    science teacher, 70, 76
    technical writer, 92, 93
experience, career success and, 127–128

F
FDA. *See* Food and Drug Administration
field notes
    atmospheric scientist, 20
    chemist/materials scientist, 64–65
    environmental scientist, 84–86
    food technologist, 109

R

related work experience
    atmospheric scientist, 18, 21
    chemist/materials scientist and, 61, 62
    environmental scientist, 82
    food technologist, 104, 105
    geoscientist, 28
    grant writer, 41
    health/safety technician, 52
    laboratory technician, 5
    technical writer, 94, 98
research assistantships, 87
resources
    atmospheric scientist, 21–22, 23
    business, starting own, 123
    chemist/materials scientists in, 66
    environmental scientist, 89
    food technologist, 109
    geoscientist, 34–35, 46
    health/safety technician, 56
    laboratory technician, 12
    science teacher, 70, 77
    technical writer, 98–99
résumé, 132–133
cover letter for, 133–134
The Riley Guide: Steps in Starting Your Own
    Business, 123

S

salary/wages
    chemist/materials scientist and, 60
    environmental scientist, 82
    food technologist, 105
    geoscientist, 27, 45
    health/safety technician, 51
    laboratory technician, 4
    technical writer, 94
science, possible career choices in, xi–xiv
science teacher, xii, 68–77

age group landmarks, 75–76
career compasses, 68
education/training, 70, 71
essential gear, 70, 76
field notes, 74–75
job description, 68–71
job prospects, 68–69
licensing/certification, 69, 72
resources, 70, 77
skills/qualifications, 71–72
transition expedition, 73–75
sixties plus age group
    atmospheric scientists in, 23
    chemist/materials scientists in, 66
    environmental scientists in, 88
    food technologists in, 109
    geoscientists in, 34
    grant writers in, 46
    health/safety technicians in, 56
    laboratory technicians in, 11
    science teachers in, 76
    technical writers in, 98
skills/qualifications
    atmospheric scientist, 15, 17–19
    chemist/materials scientist and, 61
    environmental scientist, 81, 82–83
    geoscientist, 27–28
    grant writer, 38, 39, 40–41
    health/safety technician, 50–51, 52
    laboratory technician, 2–3, 5–6
    science teacher, 71–72
    technical writer, 92, 93, 98
Small Business Administration, 123
Society for Conservation Biology, 89
Society for Technical Communication, 99
specialization
    atmospheric scientist and, 17–18, 19–20
    chemist/materials scientist and, 59, 62

environmental scientist and, 80, 86

geoscientist and, 29–30, 32

health/safety technician, 53

laboratory technician and, 3

statistics, viii

job loss, vii

Student Conservation Association, 89

success, outfitting for career, 127–137

energy/experience for, 127–128

T

Teach for America, 70, 77

technical writer, xiii, 91–100

age group landmarks, 98

career compasses, 91

education/training, 92–93, 95

essential gear, 92, 93

field notes, 96–97

job description, 91–94

job prospects, 97

related work experience, 94, 98

resources, 98–99

salary/wages, 94

skills/qualifications, 92, 93, 98

transition expedition, 98–99

telephone skills, 130–131

thirties/forties age group

atmospheric scientists in, 22

chemist/materials scientists in, 65

environmental scientists in, 88

food technologists in, 109

geoscientists in, 34

grant writers in, 44

health/safety technicians in, 56

laboratory technicians in, 11

science teachers in, 76

technical writers in, 98

transition expedition

atmospheric scientist, 19–22

chemist/materials scientist and, 62–64

environmental scientist, 86–88

food technologist, 106–107

geoscientist, 29–33

grant writer, 42–43

health/safety technician, 53–55

laboratory technician, 7, 10

science teacher, 73–75

technical writer, 98–99

twenties, age group

atmospheric scientists in, 22

chemist/materials scientists in, 64

environmental scientists in, 88

food technologists in, 107–108

geoscientists in, 33

grant writers in, 43

health/safety technicians in, 55

laboratory technicians in, 11

science teachers in, 75–76

technical writers in, 98

U

USDA. *See* Department of Agriculture, U.S.

W

Wise Geek, 46

Writers' Resources, 100